THE LESBIAN BODY

Monique Wittig

THE LESBIAN BODY

Translated from the French by
David Le Vay

BEACON PRESS   BOSTON

Beacon Press
25 Beacon Street
Boston, Massachusetts 02108

Beacon Press books are published under the auspices
of the Unitarian Universalist Association
of Congregations in North America.

92 91 90 89 88 87 86 85   8 7 6 5 4 3 2 1

Library of Congress Cataloging in Publication Data

Wittig, Monique.
  The lesbian body.

  Translation of: Le corps lesbien.
  I. Title.
PQ2683.I8C613   1986   843'.914   85-47943
ISBN 0-8070-6307-X (pbk.)

INTRODUCTION

In 1964 Monique Wittig, who was then 28, won the Prix Médicis in France with her first novel, *The Opoponax*. The poetry of its present-tense narrative and its evocative word-building immediately caught the attention of the critics and the novel with its schoolgirl heroines enjoyed a *succès d'estime*. Five years later came *Les Guérillères*, published with the admiring support of Mary McCarthy, who found this second novel 'a surprise, almost a shock . . . the only work of beauty to come out of Women's Lib.'

The schoolgirls had vanished and these girl guerillas, 'pearl-tressed, two-breasted Amazons', beautiful, brilliant and deadly, despatched the race of men and any belief in crude, automatic male supremacy. A few retreating male critics and readers uttered hoarse cries or crude words but most of them were impressed by the book's originality and the poetry of its language, even if the concepts behind it were hardly likely to please them. After reading and relishing it, wondering if in some way it could be termed a 'conceit', trying to assess the author's attitudes and also her undoubted sense of humour, I wondered too what Monique Wittig would or could write next.

In fact she strode over the dead bodies of men and devoted her next book to the female body and to relationships, especially the love-relationship, between women. Men, and all recollections of any male symbol, had ceased to exist. What was left? What were all these women going to

5

do with themselves? They were going to celebrate the female principle with an intensity that has probably never been achieved before.

A great deal has been said and written during the last twenty years about women and their place in the world. No one has explored this subject as passionately as Monique Wittig; no one has established that other world created and inhabited by women. It is no longer parallel to the male world but evolves and revolves on its own in space and time. In this book that world is endowed with the ideal beauty of the Greek islands where women once knew a culture of their own : but the starting point of life and civilization can after all only be the body.

Taken out of context, some of the narrator's invocations could seem far-fetched. Clearly they should not be considered out of their context or interpreted literally; just as nobody would isolate a few square centimetres from a painting by Picasso or Dali, or claim that the endless erotic incidents in *The 120 Days of Sodom* were intended to be realistic. Monique Wittig has chosen to celebrate the body by creating a new version of the *écorché* and the skeleton which exist not for study but for love, love which starts with the individual and extends to the whole species.

This much accepted, some readers will ask why they should have to tolerate such expressions as 'the tendon of Achillea' or the incident – inventive and amusing though it is – about the principle of 'Archimedea'. In Wittig's world they must tolerate them, otherwise they will be shut out. Such adaptations are essential in a world where language is the clue to speech, life and the body itself. 'The body of the text', the author has written, 'subsumes all the words of the female body. *The Lesbian Body* attempts to achieve the

6

affirmation of its reality. The lists of names contribute to this activity. To recite one's own body, to recite the body of the other, is to recite the word of which the book is made up. The fascination for writing the never previously written and the fascination for the unattained body proceed from the same desire.'

Monique Wittig then queries the whole concept of the personal pronoun which she maintains is impersonal, for it is by implication 'human (masculine)'.

'I' [*Je*] obliterates the fact that *elle* or *elles* are submerged in *il* or *ils*, i.e., that all the feminine persons are complementary to the masculine persons. . . . The 'I' [*Je*] who writes is alien to her own writing at every word because this 'I' [*Je*] uses a language alien to her; this 'I' [*Je*] experiences what is alien to her since this 'I' [*Je*] cannot be '*un* ecrivain'. . . . *J/e* is the symbol of the lived, rending experience which is *m/y* writing, of this cutting in two which throughout literature is the exercise of a language which does not constitute m/e as subject.

The French *Je* can be transformed on these lines, as can the French and English possessive adjective and pronoun and the reflexive pronoun, but the typographical implausibility of splitting our English monosyllabic 'I' is obvious. It has therefore been printed throughout as *I*.

David Le Vay, who is an eminent practising anatomist and surgeon, has abandoned any male chauvinism long enough to translate this book. He has pointed out that over the centuries much poetic energy has been dedicated to the outside surface of the human body, but that nobody – with the possible exception of certain contributors to the Old

7

Testament – has celebrated with such freedom the whole of the body, its skin, bones, organs, muscles, nerves, secretions and excretions, everything that adds up to *life*.

Life, yes, but is this women's world self-destructive? Sappho, unfortunately for her devotees, is rumoured to have killed herself for a man. Monique Wittig's personae are in no danger of doing that, for whatever we feel about the premise from which they start, their progress after that point reveals a frightening logic. The implications of a poetic anatomy of the female body are wider than even the male chauvinists may think. When such phrases no longer have any bitter relevance and the phrase 'two cultures' may have a sexual connotation only, *The Lesbian Body* will still provide stimulating reading, for both women and men.

Margaret Crosland

AUTHOR'S NOTE

Le Corps Lesbien has lesbianism as its theme, that is, a theme which cannot even be described as taboo, for it has no real existence in the history of literature. Male homosexual literature has a past, it has a present. The lesbians, for their part, are silent – just as all women are as women at all levels. When one has read the poems of Sappho, Radclyffe Hall's *Well of Loneliness*, the poems of Sylvia Plath and Anaïs Nin, *La Bâtarde* by Violette Leduc, one has read everything. Only the women's movement has proved capable of producing lesbian texts in a context of total rupture with masculine culture, texts written by women exclusively for women, careless of male approval. *Le Corps Lesbien* falls into this category.

The descriptions of the islands allude to the Amazons, to the islands of women, the domains of women, which formerly existed with their own culture. They also allude to the Amazons of the present and the future. We already have our islets, our islands, we are already in process of living in a culture that befits us. The Amazons are women who live among themselves, by themselves and for themselves at all the generally accepted levels : fictional, symbolic, actual. Because we are illusionary for traditional male culture we make no distinction between the three levels. Our reality is the fictional as it is socially accepted, our symbols deny the traditional symbols and are fictional for traditional male culture, and we possess an entire fiction into which we project ourselves and which is already a possible reality. It is our fiction that validates us.

The body of the text subsumes all the words of the female body. *Le Corps Lesbien* attempts to achieve the affirmation of its reality. The lists of names contribute to this activity. To recite one's own body, to recite the body of the other, is to recite the words of which the book is made up. The fascination for writing the never previously written and the fascination for the unattained body proceed from the same desire. The desire to bring the real body violently to life in the words of the book (everything that is written exists), the desire to do violence by writing to the language which *I* [*j/e*] can enter only by force. 'I' [*Je*] as a generic feminine subject can *only* enter by force into a language which is foreign to it, for all that is human (masculine) is foreign to it, the human not being feminine grammatically speaking but he [*il*] or they [*ils*]. 'I' [*Je*] conceals the sexual differences of the verbal persons while specifying them in verbal interchange. 'I' [*Je*] obliterates the fact that *elle* or *elles* are submerged in *il* or *ils*, i.e., that all the feminine persons are complementary to the masculine persons. The feminine 'I' [*Je*] who is speaking can fortunately forget this difference and assume indifferently the masculine language. But the 'I' [*Je*] who writes is driven back to her specific experience as subject. The 'I' [*Je*] who writes is alien to her own writing at every word because this 'I' [*Je*] uses a language alien to her; this 'I' [*Je*] experiences what is alien to her since this 'I' [*Je*] cannot be '*un* ecrivain'. If, in writing *je*, I adopt this language, this *je* cannot do so. *J/e* is the symbol of the lived, rending experience which is m/y writing, of this cutting in two which throughout literature is the exercise of a language which

10

does not constitute m/e as subject. *J/e* poses the ideological and historic question of feminine subjects. (Certain groups of women have proposed writing *jee* or *jeue*.) If *I* [*J/e*] examine m/y specific situation as subject in the language, *I* [*J/e*] am physically incapable of writing 'I' [*Je*], I [*J/e*] have no desire to do so.

THE LESBIAN BODY

In this dark adored adorned gehenna say your farewells m/y very beautiful one m/y very strong one m/y very indomitable one m/y very learned one m/y very ferocious one m/y very gentle one m/y best beloved to what they, the women, call affection tenderness or gracious abandon. There is not one who is unaware of what takes place here, which has no name as yet, let them seek it if they are determined to do so, let them indulge in a storm of fine rivalries, that which *I* so utterly disown, while you with siren voice entreat some woman with shining knees to come to your aid. But you know that not one will be able to bear seeing you with eyes turned up lids cut off your yellow smoking intestines spread in the hollow of your hands your tongue spat from your mouth long green strings of your bile flowing over your breasts, not one will be able to bear your low frenetic insistent laughter. The gleam of your teeth your joy your sorrow the hidden life of your viscera your blood your arteries your veins your hollow habitations your organs your nerves their rupture their spurting forth death slow decomposition stench being devoured by worms your open skull, all will be equally unbearable to her.

If some woman should speak your name *I* feel as if m/y ears were about to fall heavily to the ground, *I* feel m/y blood warming in m/y arteries, *I* perceive at a glance the networks it irrigates, a cry fit to make m/e burst issues from the depth of m/y lungs, *I* repress it with difficulty, suddenly *I* become the place of the darkest mysteries, m/y skin bristles and becomes covered with stains, *I* am the pitch that burns the assailants' heads, *I* am the knife that severs the carotid of the newborn ewe-lambs, *I* am the bullets of the submachine-guns that perforate the intestines, *I* am the pincers brought to red heat in the fire that tear the flesh, *I* am the plaited whip that flagellates the skin, *I* am the electric current that blasts and convulses the muscles, *I* am the gag that gags the mouth, *I* am the bandage that hides the eyes, *I* am the bonds that tie the hands, *I* am the mad tormentor galvanized by torture and your cries intoxicate m/e m/y best beloved the more that you restrain them. At this point *I* invoke your help m/y incomparable Sappho, give m/e by thousands the fingers that allay the wounds, give m/e the lips the tongue the saliva which draw one into the slow sweet poisoned country from which one cannot return.

I discover that your skin can be lifted layer by layer, *I* pull, it lifts off, it coils above your knees, *I* pull starting at the labia, it slides the length of the belly, fine to extreme transparency, *I* pull starting at the loins, the skin uncovers the round muscles and trapezii of the back, it peels off up to the nape of the neck, *I* arrive under your hair, m/y fingers traverse its thickness, *I* touch your skull, *I* grasp it with all m/y fingers, *I* press it, *I* gather the skin over the whole of the cranial vault, *I* tear off the skin brutally beneath the hair, *I* reveal the beauty of the shining bone traversed by blood-vessels, m/y two hands crush the vault and the occiput behind, now m/y fingers bury themselves in the cerebral convolutions, the meninges are traversed by cerebrospinal fluid flowing from all quarters, m/y hands are plunged in the soft hemispheres, *I* seek the medulla and the cerebellum tucked in somewhere underneath, now *I* hold all of you silent immobilized every cry blocked in your throat your last thoughts behind your eyes caught in m/y hands, the daylight is no purer than the depths of m/y heart m/y dearest one.

You gaze at m/e with your ten thousand eyes, you do so and it is *I*, *I* do not stir, m/y feet are completely embedded in the ground, *I* allow m/yself to be reached by your ten thousand glances or if you prefer by the single glances of your ten thousand eyes but it is not the same, such an immense gaze touches m/e everywhere, *I* hesitate to move, if *I* raise m/y arms toward the sun you slant your eyes to adjust to the light, they sparkle but you look at m/e or else if *I* should move into the shade *I* am cold your eyes are not visible there where you follow m/e *I* too am unseen by you, *I* am dumb in this desert devoid of your ten thousand eyes darker than the dark where your eyes would appear to m/e ten-thousand fold black and shining, *I* am alone until the moment when *I* hear a variety of sounds of bells of tintinnabulations, *I* tremble, *I* am giddy, it reverberates within m/e, it makes m/e quiver, it is the music of the eyes *I* say to m/yself, either they clash together gently and with violence or they produce these many sounds by themselves, *I* fling m/yself flat on m/y face in front or behind this side or that, *I* gesticulate wildly to learn that *I* cannot escape the multiplicity of your regard, wherever *I* may be m/y ineffable one you gaze at m/e with your ten thousand eyes.

I shall not utter your adorable name. Such is the interdict you have laid on m/e, so be it. *I* shall recount only how you come to seek m/e in the very depths of hell. You swim across the muddy waters of the river heedless of the semi-living lianas the roots the eyeless snakes. You sing without pause. The female guardians of the dead mollified close their gaping mouths. You obtain their permission to bring m/e back as far as the light of the living on condition that you do not turn round to look at m/e. The march along the underground passages is interminable. *I* can see your broad back one or other of your breasts when your movements show you in profile, *I* see your strong and powerful legs your straight pelvis, *I* see the hair that reaches your shoulders whose chestnut colour *I* find so beautiful to look at that a pain rises in m/y breast. You do not once turn round. The stink of m/y bowels surrounds us at m/y every movement. You seem not to notice it, you walk on steadily calling m/e in a loud voice all the love names you were used to call m/e. From time to time m/y yellow decaying arms from which long worms emerge brush against you, some climb on your back, you shudder, *I* can see your skin bristle right across your shoulders. We traverse the length of the galleries the underground tunnels the crypts the caves the catacombs you singing with victorious voice the joy of m/y recovery. M/y kneecaps appear at m/y knees from which shreds of flesh fall. M/y armpits are musty. M/y breasts are eaten away. *I* have a hole in m/y throat. The smell that escapes from m/e is noisome. You do not stop your nostrils. You do not exclaim with fright when at a given moment m/y putrescent and half-liquid body touches the length of your bare back. Not once do you turn round, not even when *I* begin to howl in despair the tears trickling down m/y gnawed cheeks to beg you to leave m/e in m/y tomb to brutally describe to you m/y decomposition the purulence of m/y eyes m/y nose m/y vulva the caries of m/y teeth the fermentation of m/y vital organs the colour of m/y rotten-ripe muscles. You interrupt m/e, you sing with strident voice your certainty of triumph over m/y death, you do not heed m/y sobs, you drag m/e to the surface of the earth where the sun is visible. Only there at the exit towards the trees and the forest do you turn to face m/e with a bound and it is true that looking into your eyes *I* revive with prodigious speed.

You are exsanguinated. All your blood torn forcibly from your limbs issues violently from your groins carotid arms temples legs ankles, the arteries are crudely severed, it involves the carotids brachials radials temporals, it involves the iliacs femorals tibials peroneals, the veins are simultaneously laid open. *I* stumble against you, *I* cannot look at you, your blood dazzles m/e, your pallor plunges m/e into confusion distraction ecstasy. So exposed your lips baring your teeth your eyes opening and closing with difficulty, your brightness eclipses the sun. A gentle wheezing issues from your mouth. Each drop of your blood each spurt from your arteries striking m/y arteries vibrates throughout m/e. *I* am unable to stir, *I* await an apotheosis a glorious end in this place where the primary colours are not lacking, *I* tremble before the bright red efflux from your arteries, *I* see it turn to black in drying stains and patches all around you and on m/y body, *I* see the dark blood emerge from the blue of your veins, in places it is congealed violet, *I* am illuminated by the gold and black of your eyes, *I* do not seek m/y life from you, *I* follow you closely, *I* hear your most precious blood as it leaves you, it makes a lancinating fabled music m/y adored one to which your voice and m/ine do not contribute.

Your hair is all black and shining. In the space between your long jaws teeth exposed *I* recognize your ambiguous infinite smile. Your tall ears move and quiver. M/y hand placed on your sweat-covered flank excites a bristling of your skin. *I* run light fingers down the length of your spine or else m/y hands bury themselves in your coat. *I* touch your firm breasts, *I* squeeze them in m/y hand. You stand upright on your paws one of them intermittently scratching the ground. Your head weighs on the nape of m/y neck, your canines gash m/y flesh where it is most sensitive, you hold m/e between your paws, you constrain m/e to lean on m/y elbows, you make m/e turn m/y back to you, your breasts press against m/y bare skin, *I* feel your hairs touching m/y buttocks at the height of your clitoris, you climb on m/e, you rip off m/y skin with the claws of your four paws, a great sweat comes over m/e hot then soon cold, a white foam spreads the length of your black chops, *I* turn around, *I* clutch at your coat, *I* take your head between m/y hands, *I* speak to you, your great tongue passes over m/y eyes, you lick m/y shoulders breasts arms belly vulva thighs, a moment comes when frenziedly you take m/e on your back m/y she-wolf m/y arms round your neck m/y breasts m/y belly against your fur m/y legs gripping your flanks m/y sex thrusting against your loins, you begin to gallop.

Happy if like Ulyssea *I* might return from a long voyage. The island's approaches are signalled to m/e before daybreak. At news of land all the women stand and prepare themselves. Not one wears the previous day's garments. The trays of perfume are laid out on the decks. There is sandalwood there is amber there is benzoin there is musk there is opoponax. They mix them with oils before spreading them over their sun-tanned skins. The trees to port and starboard are sprinkled wiped clean leaf by leaf. Some of the women attach streamers to them with the colours of the island. The masts too are laden with decorations. All the musical instruments are laid out on the deck. In the background *I* attempt to recreate your face feature by feature, *I* remain silent in the joy of m/y heart. But no *I* am well aware that *I* am not part of this voyage, *I* am on land in the most inhospitable land that exists that which does not contain you, the land you have left to make your way elsewhere. M/y feet are heavy when *I* go to the port in the evening. No sunset m/y living one will illuminate the board where the name of your ship will be inscribed. *I* can tear from m/y forehead the violet bandeau that signals m/y liberty so dearly bought as for you all m/y dearest ones *I* ask you if you love m/e to let m/e die one night far away in the sea.

M/y most delectable one *I* set about eating you, m/y tongue moistens the helix of your ear delicately gliding around, m/y tongue inserts itself in the auricle, it touches the antihelix, m/y teeth seek the lobe, they begin to gnaw at it, m/y tongue gets into your ear canal. *I* spit, *I* fill you with saliva. Having absorbed the external part of your ear *I* burst the tympanum, *I* feel the rounded hammer-bone rolling between m/y lips, m/y teeth crush it, *I* find the anvil and the stirrup-bone, *I* crunch them, *I* forage with my fingers, *I* wrench away a bone, *I* fall on the superb cochlea bone and membrane all wrapped round together, *I* devour them, *I* burst the semicircular canals, *I* ignore the mastoid, *I* make an opening into the maxilla, *I* study the interior of your cheek, *I* look at you from inside yourself, *I* lose m/yself, *I* go astray, *I* am poisoned by you who nourish m/e, *I* shrivel, *I* become quite small, now *I* am a fly, *I* block the working of your tongue, vainly you try to spit m/e out, you choke, *I* am a prisoner, *I* adhere to your pink and sticky palate, *I* apply m/y suckers to your delicious uvula.

Glorious will be the day when you come to meet m/e feet together ankles joined thrusting the clouds away from the depths of the sky with your arms your hair stirred by the wind your teeth bared and clenched with exertion your eyes regarding m/e from afar. You wear buckled on your bare hips the sword the women brought to red heat in the fire before giving it to you, the one *I* see you brandish from time to time above your head to keep off one or other hideous monster which springs up to slacken your advance. Rapture fills m/e to see you so prodigiously shoot forth your body wafting gusts of perfume towards m/e on the air-currents on this side and that pouring cataracts of sandalwood ginger hellebore and green daisies. *I* see you, you come towards m/e with adorable precipitancy, orange flashes coming from your breasts surround you, series of suns are setting in gold green saffron. Your very precise very soft very strident voice reaches m/e sooner than *I* catch sight of you causing m/e to tremble with impatience, while m/y feet are rooted in the ground, while *I* am paralysed by the suddenness of your advent, after some confusion *I* rapidly experience vertigo, m/y eyelids start to flutter incessantly over m/y eyeballs, fluttering lids are born beneath m/y hair in the depths of m/y brain, weakness takes m/y hamstrings forcing m/e to bend m/y knees, already you descend in a sustained hissing, already you stand right beside m/e, already your hands fall on m/y shoulders pressing down on m/e steadying m/e before you, already we are face to face now and for ever so be it.

Great fragments of gelatine become detached trembling transparent. The parted lips tyrian pink on the inside let the fragments pass in ever-increasing numbers. The fingers caught in the flux move slightly elongate relax draw their tips along the lips move straighten out palpate the mucous membranes with dawdling movements. The flow becomes continuous, the foamy juice whitened in its eddies rises to the shoulders, the head emerging hair spread out cheeks pale. Now the fingers tap continuously on the membranes. An agitation disturbs the flow of transparent juice fluid water. Abundant salty tears are shed into the flow, *I* drown, the water re-enters by m/y eyes juice tears, in it *I* see blacks golds lights crystals scales. *I* am seized with a great disturbance, m/y ears are lifted, buzzing bruised concussed. The fingers form palms to swim extended on either side of the great masses, they touch make contact grasp each other, the window opens abruptly under the thrust of our limbs floating on a great body of bluish lactic liquid, the water rises iodized translucent, it reaches the topmost branches of the last visible trees, it beats warmly against the legs of the swimming women, submerged up to m/y facial orifices *I* see that the liquid mass continues to increase with suspended mucus pearly elastic filaments, the golds the reds now have the same colour and consistence as the clouds, the rising wave debouches in the sky, farewell black continent of misery and suffering farewell ancient cities we are embarking for the shining radiant isles for the green Cytheras for the dark and gilded Lesbos.

26

I start to tremble without being able to stop, you m/y iniquitous one m/y inquisitress you do not release m/e, you insist that *I* talk, fear grips m/e m/y hair is shaken, the soft hemispheres of m/y brain the dura mater the cerebellum move within m/y cranium, m/y tongue uvula jaws quiver, *I* cannot keep m/y lips closed, m/y teeth chatter, m/y arteries throb in furious jerks in m/y neck groins heart, m/y eyes are compressed by their orbits, m/y intestines lurch, m/y stomach turns over, the movement spreads to all m/y muscles, the trapezii deltoids pectorals adductors sartorii the internals the externals are all shaken by spasms, the bones of m/y legs knock against each other when you do not steady them you wretch, there is a prodigious acceleration of movement to the point where freed from gravity *I* rise up, *I* maintain m/yself at your eye-level, then you m/y most infamous one you chase m/e brutally while *I* fall speechless, you hunt m/e down m/y most fierce one, you constrain m/e to cry out, you put words in m/y mouth, you whisper them in m/y ear and *I* say, no mistress, no for pity's sake, do not sell m/e, do not put m/e in irons, do not make m/y eyeballs burst, deign to call off your dogs, *I* beg you, spare m/e for just a moment longer.

THE LESBIAN BODY THE JUICE THE
SPITTLE THE SALIVA THE SNOT
THE SWEAT THE TEARS THE WAX
THE URINE THE FAECES THE
EXCREMENTS THE BLOOD THE
LYMPH THE JELLY THE WATER
THE CHYLE THE CHYME THE
HUMOURS THE SECRETIONS THE
PUS THE DISCHARGES THE SUP-
PURATIONS THE BILE THE JUICES
THE ACIDS THE FLUIDS THE
FLUXES THE FOAM THE SULPHUR
THE UREA THE MILK THE
ALBUMEN THE OXYGEN THE
FLATULENCE THE POUCHES THE
PARIETES THE MEMBRANES THE
PERITONEUM, THE OMENTUM,
THE PLEURA THE VAGINA THE
VEINS THE ARTERIES THE VESSELS
THE NERVES

Spores start from your epidermis. Your pores produce them in thousands, *I* watch the tiny explosions, *I* see how the spores descend at the end of hairy filaments without becoming detached from them, the stalks shoot, the spores develop and become rounded, the innumerable spheres clashing together create stridences clickings aeolian harp vibrations. Slowly you stand erect your arms extended before you your thighs rigid your entire body in movement, you move forward supported by the flight of the spheres expanding in the air. Your every movement produces a harmony of sounds which make the ears shift in all directions. *I* follow you, *I* move forward in your gigantic shadow scaled down prolonged by the spheres. In thousands they blur your outline or else make it appear stippled when they catch the sun in the course of their gyrations. At each of your strides you pass above several women walking. Your matchless music fixes them on the spot, then one or other seized with convulsions falls in a heap to the ground. Some begin to shriek. You superb you do not halt. *I* have difficulty in following you. Now *I* run beneath you, your jostling spheres gleaming in the sun give m/e vertigo but breathless as *I* am *I* laugh freely, *I* announce you to the immobilized ones that they may watch your coming, *I* baptise you for centuries of centuries, so be it.

Why execrable foolish one m/y dearly beloved have you turned yourself into stone when *I* love you so tenderly? Your chestnut hair has the stiffness of lead wires, your brown eyes are the glass balls of a statue, in an attempt to restore you to life *I* dash m/y head against your hard breasts, blood does not flow in your veins, air does not enter your lungs, the bile lymph bone-marrow nervous connections have all come to a halt, your vulva so pleasing to hold in m/y hands no longer quivers, your labia are rigid, your clitoris is a hard kernel, the walls of your vagina are shut tight and sealed. Thus it is for this crime that women have hunted m/e separated m/e from you to silence m/y adorable voice for you for ever. You did not wait for m/e when *I* was seeking you everywhere, *I* travelled all the islands asking if anyone had news of you. The frost the blazing sun hunger thirst the lacertions of m/y limbs m/y back the long desire for you the bitter privation, *I* cannot tell them to you since your ears are of stone, what have *I* done to these hateful ones what have you done to them that they should take such decisive action, is it possible that not one of them can change it, *I* am without arms without hands without legs without sex by your side deprived of m/y life the beating of m/y heart *I* tell m/yself in vain that you are the most adorable of statues. And yet m/y stone lover

at this moment *I* see the tears flood your cheeks, they
spurt straight from your eyes striking m/e on the forehead on the chest, a burning river spreads over m/e
vile joy and suffering you perceive m/e, you hear m/e,
you are living in this living stone at m/y mouth, *I* lay
m/yself at your feet m/y statue though you are without
smell and taste. *I* appeal to the goddess that they should
change m/e into stone m/y flank joined to your flank,
they know since Sappho has written it for eternity that
Latone and Niobe love each other with a tender love.

I see your bones covered with flesh the iliacs the knee-
caps the elbows the shoulders. *I* remove the muscles
cautiously so as not to damage them, *I* take each one
between m/y fingers the long muscles the round muscles
the short muscles, *I* pull, *I* tear them by their fibres from
their bones, *I* pile them in a heap each fragment moving
slightly quivering when *I* put it down. *I* gradually extract
the bone, *I* see it appear pearly white with reddish shreds,
I lick it, *I* caress it, *I* pumice it to polish it, *I* wait till it
has a pleasing shine, *I* watch it in its silence, *I* hear all the
cries its laying bare has cost m/e horror joy profound
sadness, *I* regard your skeleton separated from the sacs

31

the humours the viscera the hair the cheeks the mouth the eyes day of nightmare the eyes the vulva so much alive, *I* feel great pity for it and a still greater love, *I* admire the delicacy of the metacarpals and the phalanges of the fingers, *I* touch the ribs so adorably contrived, *I* am seized with desire for you, *I* drool, *I* weep, the blood exerts pressure in the ventricles of m/y heart, your bones all dry polished white bare enter m/y vision, *I* touch them, confused *I* lie down on them.

The women come running down the hill, most of them hold in their arms a small white she-monkey with large grey eyes with well-shaped ears. Some of them have stiff pigtails attached to their necks. They utter loud cries as they pass under the apple-trees laden with red fruit. The little monkeys seize the apples they are given with both hands. Their eyes blink, they look here and there uncertainly. The meeting-place occurs on either side of the river. The women of m/y group interrogate those of yours in a very loud voice. You were supposed to return with green-collared wild turtle-doves. We have none of their droppings now after the disappearance of the entire colony. You laugh, you make jokes about the metamorphosis of turtle-doves into monkeys, you speak of the fall of their wings of the scarlet wings fallen from the nests, you speak of the fête of the mutant monkeys at the base of the trees, you relate how you seized hold of them by surprise, how deprived of wings and having hardly tried out their limbs they were unable to escape you. The monkeys regard you bewildered by the cries exclamations howls laughter outbursts of voices.

You look at m/e. M/y knees give way, I make you the sign, then you let yourself fall in the water, you swim across your white soaked transparent tunic suddenly appearing the colour of your skin the rapidity of your movements producing a disturbance in the water a glimmer at the level of your shoulderblades, your monkey clinging mutely to your hair. I come to meet you, I reach you well on this side of the middle of the river our bellies our arms touching a little of your saliva trickling into m/y mouth. You attempt to wrench the little monkey from your hair to give her to m/e. But she begins to utter strident cries clinging on with her four paws, descending to your neck to clasp it with both arms. A boat passes close by seeking the women carrying the monkeys. The woman ceases rowing balancing the oars horizontally. You lie down behind her in the bottom of the boat. The little white monkey is seated between us. You suggest calling her Chloë. Above the sides of the boat the already sombre sky is visible, then the tops of the trees and the hill when we approach welcomed by shouts songs laughter. Your palm m/y best beloved separates from m/y palm.

Fire fire fire even to the tendon of Achillea the well-named she who so loved Patroclea. Indeed the muscles all catch fire simultaneously the trapezii deltoids pectorals serrati obliques recti adductors sartorii psoas. The fireball spreads between the ribs launching its eight octopus arms one tentacle gripping at once the ventricles and auricles of the heart another squeezing the aorta and the pulmonary arteries, the plexus is caught, it burns slowly, the burnt intestines disintegrate right to the tips of their villosities innumerable as they may be, their unwinding coils rest on m/y abdominal wall, m/y clitoris touched by one of the mouths is an intense irradiant irradiant sun, it creates the blowing of a forge from top to bottom of m/y body

34

raucousness issuing from m/y throat and m/y parted lips, a purple mist passes before m/y gaze, the darkness of your eyes touches m/e engulfs m/e, you appear pale, you become blurred, you become terribly diaphanous, m/y fingers make holes in you in various places m/y mere surface m/y so flat one m/y depthless one m/y veil of Lesbos your face all flat painted on the linen of Veronica like the anguished features of Christa the much-crucified.

There is no trace of you. Your face your body your silhouette are lost. In your place there is a void. In m/y body there is a pressure at the level of the belly at the level of the thorax. There is a weight on m/y chest. Initially these phenomena are intensely painful. Because of them *I* seek you but without knowing it. For instance, *I* walk beside the sea, m/y entire body is sick, m/y throat does not allow m/e to speak, *I* see the sea, *I* gaze at it, *I* search, I question m/yself in the silence in the lack of traces, *I* question an absence so strange that it makes a hole within m/y body. Then *I* know in absolutely infallible fashion that *I* am in need of you, *I* require your presence, *I* seek you, *I* implore you, *I* summon you to appear you who are featureless without hands breasts belly vulva limbs thoughts, you at the very moment when you are nothing more than a pressure an insistence within m/y body. You lie on the sea, you enter m/e by the eyes, you arrive in the air *I* breathe, *I* summon you to show yourself, *I* solicit you to emerge from this non-presence which engulfs you. Your eyes perhaps are phosphorescent, your lips are pale m/y much desired one, you torment m/e with a slow love.

Two black swans swim in the solitary lake. The golden light of the setting sun has veiled the waters. The two swans glide gently side by side, you with bent head *I* ready to support the fall of your neck to touch the curve of your breast with m/y beak. Your eyes are golden, they do not regard m/e. You allow yourself to fall behind, then unhurriedly you rejoin m/e your flank touching m/y flank, all m/y feathers ruffle to the top of m/y skull. *I* have forgotten the swans' cry of victory when they move toward the shade to rest after a day without combat. You spread your wings over m/e. *I* search their undersides with m/y beak, a slight moisture comes to m/y two respiratory orifices. Among the down *I* touch the delicate skin, *I* peck at it, you submit, then you stiffen briskly flapping your wings snapping your beak attempting a cry. Then *I* furrow your entire neck. *I* sow disorder in the arrangement of your feathers, *I* turn them the wrong way, *I* destroy their sleekness. *I* try to force you down in the water by pressing with m/y whole body on the back of yours. You resist. At a given moment you consent to glide with only head and neck emerging, *I* see them suddenly struck by the glare of the light. Of your body *I* perceive nothing a blackness merging with the black waters. *I* commence a long descent m/y neck entwining your neck dragging you dragging you down to the golden thickness of the mud from which we cannot extricate ourselves because of our firm entanglement. *I* experience the song of the black swans, at the dark hour of their death.

M/y clitoris m/y labia are touched by your hands. Through m/y vagina and m/y uterus you insert yourself breaking the membrane up to m/y intestines. Round your neck you place m/y duodenum pale-pink well-veined with blue. You unwind m/y yellow small intestine. So doing you speak of the odour of m/y damp organs, you speak of their consistence, you speak of their movements, you speak of their temperature. At this point you attempt to wrench out m/y kidneys. They resist you. You touch m/y green gallbladder. *I* have a deathly chill, *I* moan, *I* fall into an abyss, m/y head is awhirl, m/y heart is in m/y mouth, it feels as if m/y blood is all congealed in m/y arteries. You say nevertheless that you receive an enormous quantity of it on your hands. You speak of the colour of m/y organs. *I* cannot see them. *I* hear your voice hissing in m/y ears, *I* concentrate on listening to you. *I* see m/yself stretched out, all m/y entrails are unwound. *I* open m/y mouth to sing a cantata to the goddess m/y mother. M/y heart fails in this effort. *I* open m/y mouth, *I* admit your lips your tongue your palate, *I* prepare to die by your side adored monster while you cry incessantly about m/y ears.

I am laid under an interdict in the city where you live. *I* have no right to go there. The women loose your dogs on m/e when *I* approach. Everything is denied m/e, even the right of asylum. *I* am overwhelmed by desperation when *I* hear your voice saying to m/e that *I* may not come, that they are determined to prevent m/e in every way. *I* stay sitting weeping in the ditch, *I* look at the sun between the clumps of great foxgloves, it no longer appears pleasingly mauve, *I* roll in the nettles, m/y whole body is covered with blisters, a sweat of blood traverses m/y pores reddening the grass all round. *I* hear the sound of the sea against the cliffs of the island. *I* cannot raise m/y eyes to look at the village even from a distance without their being at once burned reddened affected by a bundle of white rays whose origin is unknown to m/e. M/y hair torn out by handfuls lies in heaps beside m/e. M/y cries m/y shrieks m/y ululations make your dogs shiver, they are at bay, *I* hear them whimpering, or else one or the other starts to howl at death in broad daylight. But whatever the impatience *I* provoke among them by m/y presence, they cannot prevent m/e from remaining here, they cannot compel m/e to move to a place where m/y voice would reach none of you, *I* do not even speak of you m/y best-beloved, in m/y ignorance of their actions, of their power which restrains you from running towards m/e and raising m/e up by the elbows, or else it must be that your blood is stopped in your veins by their activities, or else it is the case that you are pitiless towards m/e putting m/e to a severe test making use of them to prevent m/e from joining you immune to my sobs mouth closed blind and superbly immured in yourself.

THE PLEXUSES THE GLANDS THE
GANGLIA THE LOBES THE
MUCOSAE THE TISSUES THE
CALLOSITIES THE BONES THE
CARTILAGE THE OSTEOID THE
CARIES THE MATTER THE MARROW
THE FAT THE PHOSPHORUS THE
MERCURY THE CALCIUM THE
GLUCOSES THE IODINE THE
ORGANS THE BRAIN THE HEART
THE LIVER THE VISCERA THE
VULVA THE MYCOSES THE
FERMENTATIONS THE VILLOSITIES
THE DECAY THE NAILS THE TEETH
THE HAIRS THE HAIR THE SKIN
THE PORES THE SQUAMES THE
PELLICULES THE SCURF THE SPOTS

Your bare feet touch the blue calyces of the anemones as you walk. The pink violet white yellow snapdragons come to your calves, some as far as your thighs. Scarlet orange yellow dahlias come up to your shoulders. The crushed violet irises leave long stains on the inward of your arms. You advance along an ultramarine avenue. The bees bumble-bees butterflies expelled from the corollas you seize in passing surround you. Rays of sunlight traversing the trees touch your lips your hair your pubic hair creating a dazzling effect. The shaken lilies amaryllis arums lose the pollen from their pistils, it is yellow on your legs and on your feet, *I* see it, *I* see you naked in a drift of cut flowers red white black tulips mauve asters pink yellow columbines orange marigolds blue white pink violet michaelmas daisies pink pale-blue ultramarine cornflowers tawny brown scarlet yellow white madder-red chrysanthemums, *I* see you, you roll over and over, you rub your cheeks your belly your sex against the flower-heads, you seize them in fistfuls to cover yourself, the insects fly off buzzing around you, you laugh with mouth wide open, slowly you rock to and fro, you fall backward, you disappear completely one or other arm emerging momentarily, or there may be glimpsed the bulge of a thigh or the white gleam of your belly or your curved throat or the hair you toss all mingled with the flower-stalks, *I* look at you, *I* am unable to stir, *I* struggle, *I* am unable to reach you monster.

Am *I* not Zeyna the all-powerful she who shakes her mane and grasps the lightnings in her hand? *I* see m/yself seated rigidly before abundantly laden tables refusing all the victuals the women offer m/e calling for the drinks of Ganymedea the absent. At last you emerge hurriedly from the avenue of cherry-trees in the midst of the feast flushed breathless two amphorae supported on your straight hips eager to serve all the women who await you dry-throated, but it is by m/e that you first halt. I look at the trickle of sweat between your breasts and your lifted arms the curled damp tufts of your armpits lit by the sun, *I* grasp your straight unwaisted torso between m/y hands, you with a twist of the loins slipping from my clutch pouring a great quantity of wine into my cup. Your eyes are hidden by their lids, no blush comes to your cheeks when *I* ask you to sit beside m/e, your eyes do not see m/e, your ears do not hear m/e, the order of your gestures is undisturbed, then the fire of m/y lightnings expands in m/y breast ravaging m/y lungs m/y ribs m/y shoulderblades m/y breasts, m/y hands seizing them to thunder from the height of m/y anger, mute indifferent barely smiling you go and come soundlessly, you do not kiss the nape of m/y neck when you pass behind m/e. A growling rises in m/y throat, a rumbling develops in the cloudless sky, m/y lightnings shaken forth

42

strike you in the belly the pubis so that you turn your face to the ground before m/e m/y so frightened one m/y so troubled one your eyes closed your hands over your ears, crying to m/e for mercy in such wise that ultimately *I* can lift you at arm's length to m/y mouth, that ultimately *I* can laugh in your ears, that ultimately *I* can turn you round and bite you in the hollow of your loins m/y goddess m/y so callipygous one m/y adored.

The temperature of the island cools. A great wind takes hold of us, we are flung down. *I* see you dragged along the shingle of the beach by a violent blast, *I* clutch hold of you, *I* struggle with something an enormous flapping wing with invisible claws a kind of thing of immeasurable strength engaged in dragging you away, *I* beat the air, *I* seize you round the waist, you spin round and round, you fly off raised from the ground, you carry m/e with you, with your arms firmly grasping m/ine you pull m/e, you exert traction on m/e, your teeth are clenched, your hair is shaken out around your head, the thing seeks to reach your cheeks, *I* fight it without finding it, it lashes your shoulders, the skin of your back becomes striped with long purplish marks. *I* am filled with hatred, *I* clasp you with all m/y might, you do not let go of m/e, you hold m/e upright before you, you are on your back lying in the foul thing that cannot be seen, you become disarticulated, your bones in collision your muscles breaking off as they come up against each other, one of your legs falls torn off from the pelvis, you lose strength, you weaken, only your strong and powerful hands your arms inured to exertion continue carrying m/e, *I* try to flatten m/yself against you, *I* try to envelop you, an immense repellent force keeps m/e at a distance, *I* cry your name, *I* shriek with lips plastered to m/y teeth and jaws, the sound of m/y voice is shaky barely audible, *I* try to reach your chest and waist with m/y hands, the second leg falls off thigh torn and separated from the tibia and fibula at the knee-joint, you hold your head up with great difficulty, you struggle against the thing's movements, now there is a gigantic eddy, you waver your arms extended with increasing difficulty no longer able to support m/e, a violent gust attacks your iliac bones.

I look at you m/y unique one. You agitate the collectivity
of your vibratile cilia all over your surface. *I* approach
your flagella, m/y palms barely come into contact with
them and withdraw. A violent movement traverses you.
All your whips retract and begin to whirl, *I* do not flinch
when at the next moment they fall brutally on m/y
shoulders. The movements occur by helical rotations, *I*
am touched only cyclically. Despite your gigantic size
the length of your flagella and the speed of their propul-
sion you touch m/e with great gentleness, the silk of your
cilia makes m/e shiver from head to feet. In the furrow
of your cilia *I* perceive your wide-open mouth. The
slightest shock-wave traverses you entirely. Nowhere
within you is there a neutral circuit. *I* plug m/yself into
you, instantly your composition changes, you assume a
new shape appearance colour, a passer-by returning from
her walk would not recognize you. You move your mass
away from the point *I* touch when m/y fingers brush
against you. The more you advance precipitately towards
m/e the more you recoil rapidly and move away. Or else
you begin to spin on yourself in every direction. You are
agitated throughout by a disturbance, you hurl yourself
against the membrane which forms a sac all round you.
At a·given moment you change direction, you project
yourself abruptly towards m/e, all at once your bulk
surrounds m/e burdening m/y limbs your flagella descending the length of m/y back your mouth applied to
m/y throat, it's then my fine protozoan m/y green in-
fusorium m/y violent vorticella that slowly drawn in by
the suction of your mouth *I* faint away.

45

Unnameable one you buzz in m/y ears, the sound spreads with celerity beyond the cochlea, it gains the cerebellum, it strikes the cerebral hemispheres, it insinuates itself the whole length of the scalp so that *I* bristle with horror, it descends the spinal cord, it hammers m/y ribs, it traverses m/y lungs, *I* pant, *I* shudder. *I* tremble. *I* cannot keep m/y mouth closed, *I* cry to you, *I* call to you, you unnameable unnamed, she whose name *I* may not utter she whose unnameable name pronounced by m/e makes the wasps leave their hives, they are on m/e in swarms, they blind m/e, they strike m/e with their bodies as they fall on m/e, they stab m/e with their stings in thousands, they stun m/e with their infernal buzzing, they enter m/y ear-passages, they penetrate m/e, they burst m/y eardrums, they obstruct m/y sinuses, they inject the poison of their stings into m/y tissues, they insert your anger into m/e, cruel unnameable one call off your wasps, *I* beg for mercy, *I* am utterly consumed, long long is the fire, the poison-hoarding white demons have envenomed m/e in your name, now *I* hate you m/y most unnameable one, not once *I* swear to you will *I* utter your name.

You are face to face with m/e sphinx of clay, as I follow you eyeless grey crouched over m/e. The movements are effected noiselessly, in a broad pale nocturnal space feet touching the ground a clearing of chalky aspect where the two shapes squat observing each other insubstantial phantoms, or else moving among the clouds of the sky in the white-coloured substance of the atmosphere. From somewhere comes a long sigh a groan a moan a whimper a lamentation. The two shapes removed from each other begin to stir. *I* know by heart the place where you are, thus it is *I* make m/y way in your direction without making the least halt yet without being able to see or hear you. Fear comes to m/e immobilizing m/e. You likewise halt. A wind passes vigorously shaking the trees at the edge of the field and the flimsy bushes round about. There is an ululation. The two barely visible shapes are recumbent behind a row of shrubs. Quite a space separates them the sum of several jets of spittle. Their faces are indistinct confused at times with the general greyish light of the place. Or else when they become clear they are covered with a kind of hood identical with that worn by a falcon at the wrist. Then among their bulks there occur translations stirrings writhings swayings even glidings. *I* begin to sway before you while you are in suspense. *I* am taken with the desire to enter

47

into the darkness of your body your face your limbs. A hissing is audible. A continuous vibration traverses m/y body. *I* approach you by fits and starts, when at last *I* touch you or else it's you who does it a disturbance shakes m/e, the shock is simultaneously conveyed to you, *I* collapse from head to feet. At the moment when they come together the two sphinxes disintegrate completely, their masses crumble cave in founder totter grains of sand on grains of sand a heap very quickly forming first the heads disappearing in a flash the shoulders collapsing immediately afterwards in the same movement, you cease to exist m/y most shadowed one m/y most silent one *I* likewise.

The reflection of the moon on the sea has not been visible for a long time. A feeble white slightly bluish light smooths the confused contours of island sea land sky. The five black bitches lying half-submerged in the water on the sand slowly begin to get up opening their mouths wide shaking their fur stretching their paws their large ears pricked up on their heads. The fields of corn whose last row sprouts in the sea are uncut, the dark splashes of poppies appear in many places. Through your parted lips comes the sound of a barely audible modulated song. *I* see your teeth when your lips retract. The dark holes of your eyes are turned toward the horizon sky or sea no line marking the interval between the two. Your stiffened steaming hair is stretched straight over your head behind your ears on each side. A white vapour issues from it on all sides and envelops you down to the feet concealing the shape of your body. Sometimes in their movements your arms your hands make holes in the thickness of this mist, *I* see their gentle motions. The soles of your feet your heels are not placed on the ground. You maintain yourself slightly above the surface resting on the air, you move by glidings which seem to operate without your stirring. You are mute save for this feeble rather shrill modulation reaching m/y ears from time to time. You are seized by great activity. *I* see you abreast of the rounded bulk in the middle of the cornfield the wild rose-bush assuredly laden with red flowers visible in broad daylight. Contrariwise *I* see you suddenly above the sea where you stay motionless, *I* do not perceive you, you have passed beyond the curve of the beach, the clamour of your voice is perceptible to m/e. A sudden breeze stirs the cornfield, ruffles m/y hair, you are behind m/e, *I* am harshly aware of your presence, your breath is warm on the nape of m/y neck, the whiteness of the light is dazzling now, the water of the sea shines milky barely moving, the pale ears of corn appear, you are erect before m/e m/y most radiant one carrying the white sword of the morning your body suddenly emerged from its mist

49

your strong legs visible and the soles of your feet, you draw back and advance on m/e tall shining your cheeks adazzle. It is only m/y most powerful one when one of the women over there sings the first song of the day that you descend to step away, *I* throwing m/yself to the ground clasping your knees laughter traversing m/y lungs.

You are m/y glory of cyprine m/y tawny lilac purple one, you pursue m/e throughout m/y tunnels, your wind bursts in, you blow in m/y ears, you bellow, your cheeks are flushed, you are m/yself you are m/yself (aid m/e Sappho) you are m/yself, *I* die enveloped girdled supported impregnated by your hands infiltrated suave flux infiltrated by the rays of your fingers from labia to throat, m/y ears affected liquefy, *I* fall *I* fall, *I* drag you down in this fall this hissing spiral, speak to m/e accursed adored eddying maelstrom torment of pleasure joy joy tears of joy, *I* drag you down, your arms twined round m/e embrace two bodies lost in the silence of the infinite spheres, what am *I*, can anyone standing at her window say that she sees m/e pass, gentle muzzled suckling-lamb cat *I* spit you out *I* spit you out.

We descend directly legs together thighs together arms entwined m/y hands touching your shoulders m/y shoulders held by your hands breast against breast open mouth against open mouth, we descend slowly. The sand swirls round our ankles, suddenly it surrounds our calves. It's from then on that the descent is slowed down. At the moment your knees are reached you throw back your head, *I* see your teeth, you smile, later you look at m/e you speak to m/e without interruption. Now the sand presses on the thighs. *I* shiver with gooseflesh, *I* feel your skin stirring, your nails dig into m/y shoulders, you look at m/e, you do not stop looking at m/e, the shape of your cheeks is changed by the greatest concern. The engulfment continues steadily, the touch of the sand is soft against m/y legs. You begin to sigh. When *I* am sucked down to m/y thighs *I* start to cry out, in a few moments *I* shall be unable to touch you, m/y hands on your shoulders your neck will be unable to reach your vulva, anguish grips m/e, the tiniest grain of sand between your belly and m/ine can separate us once for all. But you fierce joyful eyes shining hold m/e against you, you press m/y back with your large hands, *I* begin to throb in m/y eyelids, *I* throb in m/y brain, *I* throb in m/y thorax, *I* throb in m/y belly, *I* throb in m/y clitoris while you speak faster and faster clasping m/e *I* clasping you clasping each other with a marvellous strength, the sand is round our waists, at a given moment your skin splits from throat to pubis, m/ine in turn from below upwards, *I* spill m/yself into you, you mingle with m/e m/y mouth fastened on your mouth your neck squeezed by m/y

51

arms, *I* feel our intestines uncoiling gliding among themselves, the sky darkens suddenly, it contains orange
gleams, the outflow of the mingled blood is not perceptible, the most severe shuddering affects you affects m/e
both together, collapsing you cry out, *I* love you m/y
dying one, your emergent head is for m/e most adorable
and most fatal, the sand touches your cheeks, m/y mouth
is filled.

I return to the city of night. The hot perfumes of the
flowers spread in coloured mists above the gardens. *I*
stroll at m/y ease. Some snatches of song are heard
coming from the terraces. Suddenly at one side of the
avenues *I* perceive trickles of your blood. It flows making
a small noise, *I* recognize it, its colour leaps to m/y eyes,
there is no other like it. Exactly parallel in a gentle wave
flows the white of your eyes. *I* can no longer stand upright. An opaque blackish haze comes before m/y eyes.
M/y ears buzz. Something that feels like a rasp adheres
to m/y lungs. In the end *I* begin to run. The pain makes
m/y eyeballs start from their orbits. *I* bend down repeatedly to pick them up groping in the sand of the main
avenue. *I* cry out with impatience, *I* search on m/y knees,
I must wipe them before putting them back in place.

THE AREOLAS THE ECCHYMOSES
THE WOUNDS THE FOLDS THE
GRAZES THE WRINKLES THE
BLISTERS THE FISSURES THE
SWELLINGS THE SUNBURN THE
BEAUTY-SPOTS THE BLACKHEADS
THE HAIR FOLLICLES THE WARTS
THE EXCRESCENCES THE PAPULES
THE SEBUM THE PIGMENTATION
THE EPIDERMIS THE DERMIS THE
CUTANEOUS NERVES THE INNER-
VATIONS THE PAPILLAE THE
NERVE NETWORKS THE NERVE-
ROOTS THE BUNDLES THE
BRANCHES THE PLEXUSES THE
MOTOR NERVES THE SENSORY THE
CERVICAL THE PNEUMOGASTRIC

Whoever has dared lay hands on you, let her show herself, let her curse the day she was born. *I* run *I* run imploring you not to die, m/y feet sink into the sand, they can barely be lifted to carry m/e, *I* go towards the sacrificial stone, the moon is not yet visible, it's not possible that you are already dead. *I* am moved to cast m/yself down on the sand of the avenue because of a pain *I* feel in m/y belly. *I* cry out with rage, calling the giraffes. They are all asleep. Not one comes near m/e gambolling so that *I* may cling to its neck. Day of wrath it were better that you were all dead.

I see you standing in the square filled with sunlight. The flies hum over the street-stalls. You turn your back on m/e. Young girls carrying large baskets pass before you. *I* approach you from behind, *I* touch your shoulder, you look at m/e, *I* make a sign for you to follow m/e, you do not acknowledge m/e, you continue to regard m/e as if *I* were a stranger. Then two of the women escort you and drag you forcibly away. You call for help. No one comes to your aid. The women continue to come and go peacefully in the marketplace. You no longer resist. You look at m/e uttering insults. The place you enter is dark, coming in from the sun one cannot distinguish anything even though the lights are lit. A woman brings low tables laden with victuals. *I* invite you to eat. You do not say a word. You sit down. You begin to eat. *I* sit opposite you regard m/e fixedly erect head high a half-smile on your lips. *I* do not tell you who *I* am. At a given moment two of the women set themselves to wash you. They anoint you with oils and perfumes of iris, of bergamot, of vetiver, of amber. Still smiling you submit. When you sit down again opposite m/e your chestnut hair glistens, your eyelids are covered with a glittering powder, your bare breast is bound with the leather straps you have always worn with m/e, they have fastened identical straps to your knees round your kneecaps. And yet you continue to look at m/e as at a stranger. Even m/y most seductive voice does not move you when *I* open m/y mouth to question you on your travels. Later the lights are extinguished save for a turned-down lamp. You strictly observe the island rules of politeness when you come to stretch out at m/y side. That is why m/y delectable one *I* proceed with the greatest jubilation when *I* arm m/y fingers with m/y iron nails, when *I* rake your back and your flanks, when at last you turn towards m/e crying m/y name.

I am mounted by you bareback. Your thighs grip m/y flanks. *I* am covered with sweat. The smell of m/y close-cropped hair wafts round. *I* feel the slipperiness of your bare perspiring skin. Your arms hold m/e by the neck. Your breasts your belly are against m/y spine. M/y skin is agitated by convulsive jerks. You knead m/y muscles with your large hands, you speak to m/e, oh so sweetly so sweetly. Then *I* stiffen m/y ears m/y nostrils quivering. M/y head is shaken tugged like a mane by your hands. *I* see obliquely the tall plants of the banks the grasses in flower the great mauve foxgloves in full luxuriance. You dig your heels into m/y belly to spur m/e on. *I* stay put. You strike m/e harder. *I* resist *I* brace m/yself. Then you arm your heels and your legs. You press into m/e with all your might voice strident, you lacerate m/y flanks with your numerous steel spikes, you flay them, you expose them to the quick, you come and go angrily from top to bottom, you cry out, you arm your hands, you rake m/y·neck, you bite m/e at the level of the trapezii, the blood flows over m/y skin from all its orifices, flies in their hundreds settle there devouring m/e. Then harassed at every point *I* launch m/yself into a furious gallop, m/y hooves violently hammer the ground, *I* neigh incessantly, *I* shriek m/y hair bristling, *I* bear you away. You hold m/e in a very tight grasp, while black from head to feet darkness filling m/y eyes *I* dash forward while you remove the weapons from your heels legs hands arms, while you cautiously work your limbs into m/y wounds.

You smile motionless. *I* am kneeling at the seashore, you, you are standing before m/e arms folded, m/y mouth opens to entreat the divine incomparable Sappho. Glittering insects pass at full speed in the light of the setting sun. One of them catches in your hair, *I* hear it buzzing. You smile motionless. The first star is visible over where dazzling the sun has disappeared. *I* entreat Sappho she who gleams more than the moon among the constellations of our heavens. *I* implore Sappho in a very loud voice. *I* ask Sappho the all-powerful to mark on your forehead as on m/ine the signs of your star. *I* solicit all-smiling Sappho to exhale over you as over m/e the breezes which make us pale when we contemplate the sky and night comes. Then *I* stand beside you facing the sea. *I* await the arrival of the comets with their smoky flashes, they are here thanks be to Sappho, the stones of your star are fallen, those which marked you above your cheek at the level of the temple with a violet seal exactly like m/y own, glory to Sappho for as long as we shall live in this dark continent.

I have swallowed your arm the weather is clear the sea warm. The sun enters m/y eyes. Your fingers form a fan in m/y oesophagus, then come together to thrust further. *I* struggle against vertigo. M/y optic nerves start under a very strong pressure. The shimmer of the light on the waves insults m/y entire body. *I* am penetrated endlessly by you, you thrust into m/e, you impale m/e, *I* begin an extremely slow journey, *I* am thronged by roarings, m/y ears lengthen, they beat furiously at the wood of the deck, they strike the sides of the boat, m/y tongue cut against m/y teeth is carried away as you descend m/e, m/y vocal cords stretched by the passage of your fingers transmit no sound, cries propagate themselves within m/y arteries incessant siren wailings alarm signals. You do not stop. *I* perceive within flattened against m/y skin the organs ranged one beside the other all distended, the green bile makes halos, the stomach hangs emptied of its acid, the liver resembles a stranded turbot, the spleen has burst, but you m/y so atrocious intractable implacable one you still descend. *I* wait for you to perforate the membrane of m/y diaphragm, *I* wait for you to touch m/y pylorus, *I* wait for you to thread m/y duodenum on your hand, an enormous cry accumulates at the centre around your arm, the pressure you exert on the sound-waves finally makes m/e explode, *I* know it by heart m/y tormentor m/y most baleful one, m/y shadowy visage sparkling with black, the sea closes over m/e, then *I* draw you down, *I* drag you down, *I* take you with m/e foundering.

You are among those women who are fêted the last day of the month the twenty-eighth, those whose periods coincide with that date. The beach is covered with ixia flowers arranged entire because of their violet spikes. Of the others the calyces corollas bulbs scales racemes bundles stems pistils petals throats have been torn off and cast on the sand. There are white red poppies pale blue wisteria pink blue ultramarine clematis blue centauries violets madder pink violet lupins saffron water-lilies mallows hyacinths arums scarlet amaryllis and many other flowers which *I* do not recognize because of their dismemberment. The women walk barefoot their entire bodies painted different colours, some are decorated with designs of butterflies birds or flowers, some jump with feet together on the heaped flowers, they exclaim that they feel soft underfoot. Most of them excitedly sing and shout. You alone are silent with no ornament other than your vast rectangular pubic fleece. You advance without evincing impatience or pleasure. You keep your eyelids above your eyeballs. You do not look at any one of them. *I* tremble that *I* may not be designated, when at nightfall the fires are lighted and are reflected in the sea, to lick your blood on the inward of your thighs along your vulva between your labia within the opposed walls of your vagina. The lot is cast against m/e, *I* am not the one.

59

You regard m/e mutely without a smile. It is another who approaches, grasps your knees squatting on her heels, wipes her damp hair against your legs, opens her mouth, head thrown back regarding you. Immediately *I* fall flat on m/y face, m/y head violently strikes the ground, *I* am seized by convulsions, m/y tears flow so copiously that *I* cannot see, sobs shake m/e as *I* restrain m/y cries. Two of the women raise m/e up and take m/e away singing m/e some song making m/e listen to their flutes and tom-toms in the cover of the pine-wood. The resinous odour makes m/e giddy, *I* feel a jolt in m/y liver, m/y sobs redouble, on m/y cheeks and neck a green vomit mingles with m/y tears drool saliva, *I* flee their laughter and their songs running as far as the sea into which *I* hurl m/yself shrieking maledictions m/y most execrable one regretting in loud and strident tones the day *I* met **you here.**

The water makes the network of m/y nerves crackle the brachial plexuses the lumbars the sacral plexuses. Outside, where the weather is damnable, your hands promptly operate on m/e. The scalpel deftly manipulated by your adorable hands has detached retracted the muscles. *I* am a spider's web of nerves exactly resembling the drawings of the anatomy texts. You say m/y beloved that you can see right through m/e. You describe to m/e the water dripping from the leaves of the trees and even their shape and even their colour. It rains on m/e, it is a music that few feminine ears are in the habit of so hearing. Forgive m/e if *I* laugh, it is so enervating so terribly enervating this rain while you, you fiddle insanely with m/e with the very tips of your fingers, *I* am touched in m/y brachial nerves m/y circumflexes m/y ulnars m/y radials m/y terminal branches, *I* insist on telling you all that that's where it's most exquisite, *I* am touched in m/y facials m/y maxillaries, at that point luminous water-spouts burst over m/e, *I* don't know whether it is the storm outside or messages from m/y brain from the eyes that *I* cannot open, hundreds of orange globes a second depart and reprecipitate there, the intensity is too great, *I* feel *I* cannot stand it, *I* faint away, but not before m/y saphenous nerves are touched, who would have believed it m/y Sappho, not before m/y great sciatics begin to move or m/y tibial nerves are seized with uncontrollable convulsions, not before *I* speak to you *I* know not what name to call you by you who at this moment place your two whole hands on m/y brachial plexuses.

THE BRACHIALS THE CIRCUM-
FLEXES THE MEDIANS THE ULNARS
THE SACRALS THE LUMBARS THE
SCIATICS THE FEMORALS, THE
SAPHENOUSES THE TIBIALS THE
PLANTARS THE PATHETICS THE
RECURRENTS THE SYMPATHETICS
THE CARDIAC THE DIAPHRAGMA-
TIC PLEXUS THE BULB THE SPINAL
THE FACIALS THE GLOSSOPHARYN-
GEAL THE OPTICS THE ACOUSTICS
THE OLFACTORIES THE NERVE-
CELLS THE GLOBULES THE RED
CORPUSCLES THE LEUCOCYTES
THE HAEMOGLOBIN THE PLASMA
THE SERUM THE VENOUS BLOOD

The wind blows from the sea. Here in the midst of the fields the gulls settle. *I* walk along a little road. Night does not come. *I* do not look at the sky. When *I* fall for the first time the women support m/e under the arms, with their aid *I* walk. Loss of consciousness flings m/e to the ground again. *I* compress m/y lips when they caress m/e and when they ply m/e with questions. *I* will not say your name. It shall not issue borne on the air, it shall not make its way outside of m/e. *I* am silent. Now *I* can walk no further. *I* am lying on the bank. The grass surrounds m/e scented cool stirred by the wind. *I* do not look at the sky. The gradually assembled features of your face do not take shape in m/y memory. *I* do not see the curve of your breast. *I* have no recollection of your arms your shoulders your back your belly. *I* am unaware that your hair when licked has a delectable taste. Your pubic hairs are not visible in their quadrangular fleece, your slender sex clitoris and hood prolonged by the winged labia are not to be seen. *I* no longer see your lungs your stomach your bones your blood-vessels. *I* am stretched out on the bank. Evening does not come. *I* ask you all if you love m/e, forget that *I* exist.

Fatal the day when *I* go to seek you in the sweet-smelling sea your gaze sliding over m/y shoulders and along m/y flanks. *I* approach you quite suddenly, m/y hand touches your blue glossy skin, a shudder seizes you from head to tail the water agitated furiously all round. *I* commence a long ululation when your flank adheres to m/y flank, when *I* clasp you with both hands m/y legs entwining you beneath your white belly m/y knees squeezing you on either side. You drag m/e in your rapid progress, m/y hair spreads away from m/y head, *I* do not see the sky inverted in the depths of the waters. A glaucous light surrounds you with a green halo. The whites of your eyes are not to be seen. While *I* grasp you at the throat m/y arms clasped round your neck, *I* suddenly perceive the portcullis of your teeth your wide-open mouth. *I* am seized by weakness in m/y armpits and m/y limbs. Your teeth unclench only to tear m/e to pieces tearing off now an arm now a breast now part of m/y cheek leaving m/y face denuded of its muscles bones exposed, already *I* no longer have strength to cry out, already m/y blood flows in long red streaks visible in the water, it makes you all the more bent on m/y massacre m/y beautiful accursed shark, you reject m/e despite m/y supplications, and retreating into the distance you charge at m/e, m/y head splits, *I* see you more and more immense silent above m/e. One of m/y eyes slowly disappears and sinks milkily without rotating. You lash m/e with your tail in your comings and goings, m/y face is struck on either side, m/y hands no longer able to raise themselves to protect m/y cheeks, all m/y scattered torn fragments are gathered

by you and frenziedly devoured, *I* see you silently relish
some flakes of m/y flesh in your teeth, *I*'ve done with
watching you m/y eater of ordure m/y most nefarious one
m/y so disquieting one, happy if *I* can remain a reflection
that disturbs your gliding through the water.

I watch you, *I* watch you, *I* cannot refrain from crying
out, your face has become inert, your cheeks pale in the
extreme, sweat forms on the skin of your belly your
shoulders your loins, suddenly it covers your brow, your
hair is damp both in your armpit and at your pubis,
your lips do not move, they have a fixed smile, your eyes
turn up, your body stiffens, your muscles convulse, your
hands are clenched, you sigh lengthily, at last you collapse, *I* am seized throughout with anguish, *I* shriek, *I*
weep, *I* shake you, you do not stir, *I* call on you by the
sweetest names *I* can find, *I* kiss your wrists the inward
of your arms your nape your feet, *I* cause m/y saliva to
flow inside your mouth, *I* eat your hair, *I* scrape with
m/y teeth at the skin of your cranium, *I* lick you from
head to foot mouth slack, m/y tongue licks your knees licks
your thighs licks your vulva licks your belly licks your

breasts licks your shoulders licks your neck licks your
chin licks your closed lips, *I* take your hands all cold in
m/y hands, *I* loosen the fingers one by one, *I* weep, *I*
look at you lying beside you, *I* am beset with such great
pain and still greater love that *I* experience repeated
orgasms in great agitation, then all alive you look at m/e,
you laugh, you speak again you most savage of the
savages m/y so mad one.

You have placed your either arm around their necks. You
progress seated carried by the women on their crossed
arms. Your knees and your armpits are painted. Leather
thongs girdle your torso your waist your arms leaving
your forearms breasts belly bare. You hold yourself erect.
You look straight in front of you. You sing mouth closed
voice tenuous and modulated. Some of the women leaping around you take up the tonality in voices of different
pitch and fall back erect heels together digging a hole in
the sand of the avenue. Your bearers begin to spin slowly
at first then faster and faster, their upswept hair is
horizontal. You, you extend your arms behind their necks
your voice rises, your mouth exposes your teeth. When

the women breathless come to a halt you begin to laugh
very loudly head thrown back the curve of your throat
exposed. They put you down without roughness standing
beneath the tree with the slanting trunk an acacia whose
flowers have a heady perfume. *I* am she who has been
present motionless at the performance. *I* throw m/yself
at your knees, *I* clasp them one of m/y arms behind your
knees the other behind your calves m/y mouth coming
and going from the birth of your thighs to your round
knee-caps m/y lips applied m/y tongue moistening you
with saliva to make the rosiness of your knees shine. *I* sit
back on m/y haunches to assess the shininess. You bend
forwards your hands resting on m/y hair, you draw m/e
to you, you attempt to raise m/e up. Clinging to your
legs *I* resist m/y pressure on your hams making you give
at the knees. You do not fall. Now you are holding yourself very stiff. *I* descend the length of your legs touched
by m/y hair. M/y head rests on your feet m/y hair
spreads over their bare toes, m/y arms stretch on either
side of your legs right behind you, sharply they embrace
your ankles approximating them while you brace yourself
increasingly. Flowers torn from the acacia by the wind
fall on us their perfume stimulated by the tree's motion
invading m/e. *I* am seized with shuddering before you
so silent. The sound of the sea is heard. The women run
and chase each other on the beach. Now they can barely
be seen. You are alone as *I* am with you face to face.

I have access to your glottis and your larynx red with blood voice stifled. *I* reach your trachea, *I* embed m/yself as far as your left lung, there m/y so delicate one *I* place m/y two hands on the pale pink bland mass touched it unfolds somewhat, it moves fanwise, m/y knees flex, *I* gather into m/y mouth your entire reserves of air. Mixed with it are traces of smoke, odours of herbs, the scent of a flower, irises it seems to m/e, the lung begins to beat, it gives a jump while the tears flow from your wide-open eyes, you trap m/y mouth like a cupping-glass on the sticky mass of your lung, large soft sticky fragments insinuate themselves between m/y lips, shape themselves to m/y palate, the entire mass is engulfed in m/y open mouth, m/y tongue is caught in an indescribable glue, a jelly descends towards m/y glottis, m/y tongue recoils, *I* choke and you choke without a cry, at this moment m/y most pleasing of all women it is impossible to conceive a more magistral a more inevitable coupling.

On the hillside the women do round dances in the evening. Often and often *I* look at them without daring to approach. *I* know them all by their names from having studied them in the library books. *I* list their attributes, *I* consider their bearing, *I* am not sorry that their severity should have remain attached to the books since they are here before m/e so totally devoid of it. M/y heart beats at times when *I* see you among them m/y best beloved m/y unnameable one you whom *I* desire from the bottom of m/y stomach shall never die. *I* watch you holding the hand of Artemis laced in leather over her bare breasts then that of Aphrodite, the black goddess with the flat belly. There is also the triple Persephone, there is sun-headed Ishtar, there is Albina eldest of the Danaïds, there is Epone the great horsewoman, there is Leucippa whose mare runs in the meadow below white and shining, there is dark Isis, there is red Hecate, there are Pomona and Flora holding each other by the hand, there is Andromeda of the fleet foot, there is blonde Cybele, there is Io with the white cow, there are Niobe and Latone intertwined, there is Sappho of the violet breasts, there is Gurinno the swift runner, there is Ceres with the corn in her hair, there is white Leucothea, there is moon-headed Rhamnusis, you all dance, you all beat the ground with the soles of your feet with increasing force. None seems fatigued, while Minerva the daughter of Zeyna blows her flute and Attis beloved of Sappho beats the tom-tom. If amongst all of them you are the only one to perspire it bedecks you m/y unique one, their complaisant fingers touch you, then you shine with many fires, rays leave

69

your body descending to the ground, hammered for the nth time. *I* am troubled to see you at your ease among the women eyes shining loins twisted by spasms your pelvis thrust forward in the rhythm of the dance. Amicably you share the sacred mushroom, each one bites the edge of the cap, no one asks to become bigger or smaller. At a sign from blessed Aphrodite all around you exchange their colours. Leucothea becomes the black one, Demeter the white, Isis the fair one, Io the red, Artemis the green, Sappho the golden, Persephone the violet, the transformations spread from one to the other, the rainbow of the prism passes across their faces while you unchanging in the chestnut colour of your hair you start to cry out while *I* regard you in your great ecstasy though deprived of the sacred mushroom awaiting you in the laurels with their hidden flower and you come near m/e at one moment or another.

I take you by surprise, *I* tackle you, *I* take possession of you, *I* bear you off into the cavern all afire with the mauve violet pink lights of the lanterns. You resist, you struggle, you cry out in a strident voice. The door of the cavern glides noiselessly. You are laid down on the beaten earth at the threshold. Some women appear from the oblique corridors and holding you firmly remove your clothes. One of them having playfully placed her two hands on your mouth because of your cries is immediately bitten. You throw your head back, you shake it from side to side, you cease struggling only when they begin to massage you, then the anger leaves your eyes. Standing motionless *I* watch you. You pose no question. Four of the women bring the great silver tub full of steaming water. They plunge you in it, they wash you, they remove the traces of dust and dirt on your skin. They envelop you in large bath wraps, they perfume you, they anoint you, they comb you, give you a clean garment. Now *I* take you by the hand and draw you down on to the thick carpets. You sit on your heels, you rest your hands fingers spread on your thighs, you regard m/e in silence you do not recognize m/e. A full censer swings.

The soil of the garden slides between your teeth, your saliva moistens it, you feed m/e with it your tongue in m/y mouth your hands on m/y cheeks holding m/e still, *I* am transformed into mud m/y legs m/y sex m/y thighs m/y belly standing between your legs glutted with the smell of the vaginal secretion rising from your middle, *I* liquefy within and without. The mud reaches the muscles of m/y thighs, it touches m/y sex, it coats m/e cold and slippery, m/y labia retracting it spreads to m/y abdomen m/y kidneys m/y shoulderblades the nape of m/y neck which is circumvented in its turn, m/y neck bows, you still holding m/y cheeks in your hands filling m/e with saliva and earth your tongue against m/y gums. M/y muscles separate from each other in sodden masses. M/y entire body is overwhelmed. First to fall is m/y anus. Some glutei soon follow. M/y biceps abandon m/y arms. The arms themselves fall entire to the ground. Only m/y cheeks remain intact. A very strong smell of moist earth spreads around. *I* see plants rooted in the fibres of m/y muscles. *I* lose heart, *I* submit m/yself to your will m/y deplorable one *I* have no share in this systematic transformation you impose on m/e.

I have long been prepared for this phenomenon by various palpitations traversing m/y body at every instant. An urgent wave descends emitted by m/y brain under the touch of your fingers on m/y shoulders. M/y back opens between the shoulderblades to release the fan-shaped membranes compressed by the ribs. Violet and translucent they at once unfold and begin to quiver. You excite a new wave, your fingers arrest it at the level of m/y carotid. Now there is the gentle sound of a circular wing in process of beating, it surrounds m/y opened neck round to the nape where it is attached. It extends over m/y breasts its black veins visible in the deep mauve of the stretched skin. The unfolded beating wings brush against you not preventing you from drawing near, one of them passes over your cheeks, another makes you close your eyes. M/y brain assailed produces increasingly rapid waves. The wings are born incessantly with ever-increasing speed. M/y arms are attached to m/y sides by two gigantic wings of a black colour, once folded they are no thicker than a knife-blade, their substance is identical with that silk flags are made of. Their shape is comparable to that of the wings of bats. Each of m/y ribs is the shank of a newly-created wing. Arranged in parallel the closed wings seen in profile resemble the antennae of a lamelli-corn. Outspread they begin to rustle exposing the dull gleam of their indigo pink mauve violet colour. You stand opposite lashed by their rapid flapping your arms protecting your face eyes open. The multiplication proceeds the wings now extend as far as m/y hips, at m/y feet two membranes arise and open at once diaphanous violet palpitant transmitting waves. A quiet hissing issues from your throat while *I* stay motionless body petrified before you wings all outspread traversed throughout by vertiginous movements which at this moment make you cry out, while sombrely m/y so desired one *I* enfold you.

Be seated firmly on your heels m/y dearest one, let your thighs be of bronze, your knees of red mud of clay, your adorable hands opposed to your vasti externi whether they be gold amethyst liquid mercury, let your breast be green and shining of the same consistence as the underside of the leaves of trees, let your bust be of tempered steel, your shoulders of copper, let your loins be iron, your neck silver, your nape tin, let your cheeks be platinum, let your eyes m/y favoured one be of lead of molten lead and milk, let your vulva be of fiery infusible violent iridium, let your vulva – labia heart clitoris iris crocus – be of odorous refractory osmium, be strong m/y most beautiful one the most febrile the most flagrant m/y hands breaking on touching you m/y voice seeking to re-echo your voice.

M/y hand presses in insistent fashion at the top of your left cheek at the place where the skin is marked by the violet scar, *I* succeed thus in making your eyeball topple out, *I* watch it hanging, *I* am gripped simultaneously by emotion in the throat and by the pleasure of seeing behind your eye. At once *I* test the elasticity of the optic nerve by pulling on your eyeball with m/y fingers but without letting go. The muscular hinges that allow your eyeball to move fascinate m/e so much that *I* insert m/y tongue at the points where they are attached to the internal nerve and external nerve by a single knot. In these movements *I* touch the part of your eyeball which is normally hidden, *I* spread m/y saliva over it, *I* lick it *I* take it between m/y lips, *I* squeeze it, *I* make it roll entire within m/y mouth, *I* suck it, *I* suckle at it, *I* swallow it, *I* find m/yself connected with your optic nerve by suction, *I* apply m/yself to the orbital aperture like a cupping-glass, *I* am absorbed, *I* introduce m/yself into the motor centres behind your eye, *I* insert m/yself m/y mouth m/y tongue m/y fingers, *I* pass behind your mirror, *I* spread out, *I* embed m/yself, finally *I* reach the left hemisphere of your brain, you repel m/e with all your will-power, now *I* cling on with both hands, under m/y frantic pressure your head becomes detached at the level of the cervical vertebrae, it is immediately swept away by a violent gust of wind, *I* do not let go of you, you carry m/e with you suspended from your jugular veins in space grasped by your upswept hair m/y adorable one your mouth wide-open.

THE ARTERIAL BLOOD THE AORTIC
BLOOD THE VENULES THE
ARTERIOLES THE CAPILLARY VES-
SELS THE AORTA THE CAROTID
THE CEPHALIC THE JUGULAR THE
CORONARY THE OESOPHAGEAL
THE PULMONARY THE FACIAL THE
TEMPORAL THE SUBCLAVIAN THE
MAMMARY THE BRACHIAL THE
MESENTERIC THE RENAL THE LUM-
BAR THE ILIAC THE SACRAL THE
RADIAL THE SAPHENOUS THE
TIBIALS THE VENA CAVA THE
PORTAL VEIN THE PULMONARY
THE COAGULATION THE CLOTTING
THE CONCRETIONS THE CLOTS
THE SOLIDIFICATIONS

The city where you live is surrounded by a labyrinth where the unaccredited are lost who do not announce themselves by blowing the siren-voiced crescent-shaped trumpet fastened across the breasts by a leather thong as you all do. For a long time now *I* have been walking seeking to find the way in each of the slanting paths overcome by the scent of the flowers determined not to raise m/y trumpet to m/y mouth to rejoin you in the utmost secrecy. Grey-headed finches with blue bellies are ranked one against the other on the spreading branches of the limes at hand's height. *I* have so often traversed this garden eyes bandaged you holding m/e by the shoulders to guide m/e refusing whenever *I* asked you to give m/e a clue to m/y whereabouts. *I* recall your bites on the nape of m/y neck, the distress that afflicts m/e each time you halt leaving m/e alone in the dark, *I* recall your laughter m/y confusion when the bandage removed *I* have lost sight of you, *I* recall the torment that seizes m/e waiting for you seeking you along the sandy paths, *I* recall the cries you wrench from m/e surprising m/e from behind the persistence with which you continue to put the bandage round m/e forbidding m/e to discover how to arrive alone. Now *I* have lost heart, *I* stay seated in a grove of pink lilac. At a given moment some little girls in the treetops amuse themselves by throwing oranges at m/e. They answer m/y pleas with mockery. *I* start off again, *I* see island dwellings clearly visible in apparently quitè accessible places, *I* see them withdraw whenever *I* approach them. *I* lose patience at m/y inability to draw near them on this horizontal surface where every

77

point seems given at the first glance. A moment comes towards evening when m/y legs can no longer carry m/e, then *I* lie down bringing the coiled trumpet to m/y mouth to announce m/y surrender and fall asleep.

The bandage keeps m/y eyes closed. *I* am in darkness. A glitter sometimes an orange dazzle enters between m/y eyelids and m/y eyes firmly pressed on by the ligature. From time to time you m/y best-beloved you increase the pressure by applying your two palms to m/y eyeballs and rolling them under your fingers. A great shudder seizes m/e in the flawless night in which *I* am plunged, m/y thighs m/y legs m/y ankles are pervaded by a tingling, m/y sex especially is smarting, tiny movements take place on m/y belly, there is a pullulation on m/y breasts, the movements invade m/y skin by thousands, an increasingly intolerable formication spreads over m/e, it affects m/e up to the armpits, m/y arms are involved on both their aspects, it gains m/y neck m/y shoulders, m/y mouth 'm/y flanks are assailed. *I* have gooseflesh over m/y entire surface. Suddenly *I* am perforated by bites in numerous places where m/y skin has been touched. Then you, you begin to sing in a very soft voice m/y ravisher while *I* am no longer able to remain still, *I* begin to struggle, while *I* perceive the movements with heightened intensity. The bandage is suddenly removed by your hands. *I* discover that *I* am absolutely covered over m/y entire naked body with great black spiders from the feet to the hair m/y skin all eaten away creviced full of bites of purplish swellings vile. Your fingers rest on m/y mouth brushing away several of the creatures to prevent m/e from crying out. You look at m/e, you smile at m/e infinitely, m/y eyes are apposed to your eyes, *I* am seized by unnameable joy and horror, thus *I* abase m/yself m/y head supported by your hands.

The women lead m/e to your scattered fragments, there is an arm, there is a foot, the neck and head are together, your eyelids are closed, your detached ears are some-where, your eyeballs have rolled in the mud, *I* see them side by side, your fingers have been cut off and thrown to one side, *I* perceive your pelvis, your bust is elsewhere,

79

several fragments of forearms the thighs and tibiae are missing. M/y vision blurs at this sight, the women support m/e under the shoulders, m/y knees give way, m/y cries are stiffled in m/y breast, they ask m/e where you should be interred in what order to collect your fragments which makes m/e recoil shrieking, *I* pronounce a ban on the recording of your death so that the traitress responsible for your being torn to pieces may not be alerted. *I* announce that you are here alive though cut to pieces, *I* search hastily for your fragments in the mud, m/y nails scrabble at the small stones and pebbles, *I* find your nose a part of your vulva your labia your clitoris, *I* find your ears one tibia then the other, *I* assemble you part by part, *I* reconstruct you, *I* put your eyes back in place, *I* appose the separated skin edge to edge, *I* hurriedly produce tears vaginal juice saliva in the requisite amount, *I* smear you with them at all your lacerations, *I* put m/y breath in your mouth, *I* warm your ears your hands your breasts, *I* introduce all m/y air into your lungs, *I* stand erect to sing, far off *I* perceive the island shore and the sun shining on the sea, *I* turn away the goddesses of death squatting on their heels around you, *I* begin a violent dance around your body, m/y heels dig into the ground, *I* arrange your hair on the clumps of grass, *I* Isis the all-powerful *I* decree that you live as in the past Osiris m/y most cherished m/y most enfeebled *I* say that as in the past we shall succeed together in making the little girls who will come after us, then you m/y Osiris m/y most beautiful you smile at m/e undone exhausted.

Your palms are against m/y palms a faintness overcomes
m/e, weakness affects the hollows of m/y knees, you are
face to face with m/e the soft inward of your arms
pressed against m/y arms, then a formication spreads in
m/y epidermis, *I* see m/y pores dilate, *I* see your pores
do likewise, open they secrete fine hairs in thousands the
colour and consistence of those of the crania, they grow
at full speed, *I* feel them fall from your arms on to m/y
arms, *I* cannot distinguish yours from m/ine they are so
mingled as they multiply, the two faces remain naked,
but they develop below the chin on the shoulders on the
breasts the back, the arms the forearms are covered with
them, they emerge from the breasts, they emerge from
the loins, they emerge from the bellies thighs legs, they
reach our feet, only the vulvas and the pubic fleeces are
unaltered, they are so numerous that they create the
effect of a pelt with very long hairs of tenuous consistence,
I clasp you m/y hands buried in your hairs, *I* begin to
weep because *I* can no longer touch your bare skin. You
on the contrary you laugh, you bend m/e in your arms,
you show m/e how to catch the wind, you seek a current,
all the hairs stretch out on either side, they raise us up,
they enable us to fly away, *I* wipe m/y tears against you
m/y furred one, *I* float m/y arms on your arms, the
wind mingles our hairs, it combs them, it brushes them,

it gives them lustre, farewell dark continent you steer for the isle of the living.

The tears flow fast on your cheeks, m/y hands repair there and are moistened there, the tears fall larger and larger tepid salt against m/y mouth, they cover your neck your shoulders your breasts, *I* scatter them, *I* disperse them over your entire body, the tears continue to flow, your breast heaves with sobs, you begin to hiccup, the saliva falls in great strings from your mouth, *I* hold its elastic substance between m/y fingers, *I* carry it on m/y mouth on m/y forehead on m/y eyes on m/y cheeks, *I* stop breathing, *I* roll you in your own tears, now they make quite a pool around you, incessantly *I* utter words to make you redouble your tears, you weep without stopping, you weep for yourself, you weep for m/e with marvellous force, your entire body is involved, your shoulders heave, now you start you sob you cry out, your tears fall all at once when you straighten your neck, you implore m/e with strident voice but *I* remain utterly ferocious towards you, then you begin to weep harder still, you make yourself drunk and you intoxicate m/e while your water m/y intemperate mistress, m/y most tormented one, descends in runnels across the beach of the island to the sea.

At the first crescent of the rising moon the women make
holiday. The moonlight barely creates a reflection in the
dark eddies of the sea. The blue of the sky where several
stars are visible is paler shining and trembling round
them. *I* nar..e them in a loud voice. A lapping disturbs
the silence then ceasing re-establishes it. A warm gust
enters m/y lungs. The boats are ranged side by side. *I*
recognize your boat next to m/ine swaying poised your
flank bumping m/y flank, our two masses darker than
the others because of their black colour the violet insignia
invisible at this hour. Coming from the interior of the
island the women approach the seashore in groups bearing lanterns and hollowed pumpkins with a flame barely
stirred by the wind lighting their orange interiors. Some
of them beat the drums. The majority are covered with
garlands of flowers on their breasts round their arms, only
the colour of the white flowers adopted by those who are
black-skinned is visible, the red orange violet pink parma
are black, they make moving stains on the white-skinned
bodies. Some women blow very strident airs on flutes.
Some wear on their heads silver jewels in the form of a
crescent. Others beat in their hands dancing as they move
forward. There are those who are silent two by two well
away from the middle of the procession holding each
other by the hand. Great circles form on the beach, white

candles are grouped very closely together in complex arrangements which cover extensive areas. At a given moment the entire beach is invested. Not one empty dark spot remains, thousands of candles burn buried in the sand. The women move from one shape to another altering some details in their arrangement. You are not in any group. *I* have long since abandoned the extreme edge of the sea, there where the waves dampen the sand and make it shine. *I* seek you. You do not appear. Not one flashing moving flame illuminates your sharp features your pale cheeks your ambiguous smile. *I* am erect once more, *I* regard the sea. It is then *I* notice you, *I* do not doubt that it is you, right out at sea lying on the water in the reflection of the moon arms stretched out on either side of your pale body. *I* walk in the sea the water coming half-way up m/y body then covering m/y shoulders. *I* swim strongly over to where you are, *I* stretch out beside you, *I* hear you singing incessantly m/y exultant one you do not look at m/e, no more do *I* at you. As the night wears on the women over there draw near and cast their garlands on the sea.

Black is the brook suddenly dividing your body in two thighs disjointed at their middle knees taut breasted torso in its two parts, the left alone retaining the aorta ventricles auricles the heart in its entirety. Violet is the water of the jet surging behind the cranium round the lobes of your brain. Gold is the river issuing from your eyes, its divers effluents irrigating your shoulders and arms. *I* see the movement of the little crests, a saliva comes to your lips half-open mouth, a foam passes between your teeth, a hoarseness reaches your high throat. *I* inform you that the wooden boats the windmills the bridges manufactured by the little girls stud your suddenly closed eyes. A song is born in m/y breast to accompany the slow glidings of m/y boat across you, *I* sing the eddies which make it deviate the sharp shards of light through the trees the milky sun falling on your pale breasts the ambiguous silent laughter on your parted lips the black violet golden precipitations of the current against your vulva the tranquil medusae outspread on your palms, asleep. Black is the jet necklace across your breast passing beneath your breasts surrounding them the polished spheres of pearls now loose rolling within your mouth your bared teeth all black exposing their rapid transmutation black black stream congealed shining.

You turn m/e inside out, *I* am a glove in your hands, gently firmly inexorably holding m/y throat in your palm, *I* struggle, *I* am frantic, *I* enjoy fear, you count the veins and the arteries, you retract them to one side, you reach the vital organs, you breathe into m/y lungs through m/y mouth, *I* stifle, you hold the long tubes of the viscera, you unfold them, you uncoil them, you slide them round your neck, slopping you let them go, you cry out, you say delightful stink, you rave, you seek the green fluid of the bile, you plunge your fingers into the stomach, you cry out, you take the heart in your mouth, you lick it for a long time, your tongue playing with the coronary arteries, you take it in your hands, *I* cannot speak, your teeth biting m/y cheeks your lips unscathed at the edge of m/y lips you, your sovereign hair over m/y face, bent over you look, you, your eyes not quitting m/y eyes, covered with liquids acids chewed digested nourishment, you full of juices corroded in an odour of dung and urine crawl up to m/y carotid in order to sever it. Glory.

I find support for m/y arms on the gust of air under the trees where it blows most strongly. M/y forearms are raised, they return very quickly against m/y body, then they are raised anew, they fall back, and so on in sequence with the fingers of m/y hands outspread. At a given moment, all together, *I* take off from the ground, *I* feel the grass brush against m/y calves, at last *I* make it, *I* fly off, *I* follow the rising current which bears m/e up without m/y having to make any exertion other than to flap m/y forearms at full speed. This becomes easier as *I* establish the proper inclination of m/y trunk and pelvis. M/y legs are together. *I* look at the clouds at the place where the sun fringes them. It is there *I* direct m/yself. *I* am hardly out of breath. As soon as *I* have gained height *I* let m/yself go arms and legs extended lying on the air, *I* see the fields, *I* see the river, *I* see the clouds below m/e. *I* enter into a cold cumulus which at once soaks m/e. Then *I* flap m/y arms, *I* begin to fly lengthily endlessly on the sunny aspect lips compressed, *I* do not call your name m/y most forbidden one, the syllables would be lost in the whistling howling creaking ululation of the wind. *I* content m/yself with flying always further away from you.

THE CONGEALINGS THE CALCULI
THE STONES THE NODULES THE IN-
DURATIONS THE LAYERS THE
SCALES THE FIBRES THE FIBRILS
THE LIGAMENTS THE TENDONS
THE EXTENSORS THE SUSPENSOR-
IES THE FLEXORS THE ADDUCT-
ORS THE ABDUCTORS THE
SYNERGISTS THE ANTAGONISTS
THE TENSORS THE ROTATORS THE
ACCESSORIES THE RECTI THE
OBLIQUES THE ORBICULARS THE
TRANSVERSE THE SPHINCTERS
THE VISCERAL MUSCLES THE
SMOOTH MUSCLES THE CARDIAC
MUSCLE THE SKELETAL MUSCLES
THE TRAPEZII THE PECTORALS

M/y fingers grow at a crazy speed each of them reaching a length fifteen times greater than its original length. *I* abandon m/yself to a gentle exploration of your body at first uncertain insidious then increasingly insistent. You cry out, you utter all the words indicative of surprise pain joy circulating from m/y ear-flaps to the deepest convolutions of m/y brain traversing them in all directions. The surest of m/y fingers the index insinuates itself along your rectum, uncompressed as far as the colon it forces a passage through the faeces, it reaches the bend of the intestine, it enlarges, it turns twice on itself, it descends the length of the ascending colon, it bends again, it gains the ileum of the small intestine making almost a complete circle girdling the small intestine like a lasso. Simultaneously the middle finger is inserted into the neck of your uterus, it traverses the womb, it perforates the bowel-wall introducing itself into the small intestine. Deranged thus through and through you have stopped protesting, you are completely immobilized transfixed, you faint repeatedly. Then *I* address you, *I* demand that you ask m/e to continue, you do so, however your stomach revolts, the vomitings that reach your belly are absorbed by m/e accordingly as *I* wipe your skin with m/y tongue with m/y lips. M/y ring and little fingers remaining outside you having grown together with the other fingers are engaged in caressing your loins your shoulders your nape while *I* pursue m/y slow inexorable invasion of you. M/y two fingers within you have come together, they attempt the passage from the duodenum from the stomach to your oesophagus, *I* try to reach your

89

throat, then your mouth, from within, *I* seek to be absorbed by you during m/y writhings in your interior to be spat out rejected vomited entirely, *I* implore you in a very low voice, vomit m/e with all your might muzzled suckling-lamb queen cat spit m/e out, vomit m/e up.

It is not the gentle sound of the rain that *I* hear just now, but your blood falling on the metal, it spurts from the seven openings, the temporal arteries are severed, the carotid is cut through, the iliac arteries the radials are holed, *I* am spattered from top to toe. Your blood deserts its circuits. *I* am inundated, glory, a great mist descends from you on m/e, the heavy beating of your heart the hurrying of your aorta cradle m/e, they make m/e fall into a lethargy, a pallor overcomes you, you smile ineffable untouchable as yet untouched. *I* am gripped with fear of losing you of failing to reach you. Bending over the metal mirror *I* feverishly seek the openings to make at the temples the carotid the groins the wrists, you can do no more for m/e, you raise your eyelids in order to look at m/e, *I* beg you to wait for m/e, *I* summon you, *I* call in your ears, *I* follow you in your journey, the blood spurts from m/y badly sectioned arteries, *I* become impatient, *I* cut m/yself to pieces in m/y haste, a buzzing comes and goes from m/y chest to m/y temples, *I* seek you in the bleeding glory of the sun, *I* come m/y adored one *I* follow you *I* come to you *I* draw near you, *I* have forced the passage, then m/y blood mingles with yours inundating you entirely, the inwards of our arms finding and pressing each other, ultimately desire finds us, we move towards each other in great travail.

Your scales are so apposed that your skin resembles hard and shining metal. *I* enjoy stroking your spherical surface, *I* turn you around, you are so big m/y most adored one that *I* cannot form an overall perception of you. *I* move to the level of your eyes each of them having the breadth of thirty of m/y own. *I* pass m/y hand between the superimposed corollas which surround them. *I* cannot look at you face to face. *I* see each of your eyes in turn. One of the two yellow watches m/e, *I* begin to stagger. Your delicate gigantic mouth opens and shuts incessantly, I press m/y naked belly against it and against it and against the single lip that bounds it, your soft cold touch makes m/e shiver. *I* move under your white belly,

I press m/y hands and m/y bare feet against its slippery surface, *I* swim the whole length of your body, *I* re-ascend, *I* touch one of the small fins at the level of one of your eyes, *I* try to unfold it, it resists, it palpitates under m/y pressure. *I* let m/yself sway on your flank from one great flipper to the other, *I* try to stay balanced while you move forward at full speed. Then *I* fall in front of you at mouth level. You in the incessant movement of your single gaping curled lip m/y mole you swallow m/e, at once *I* enter into your immense red illuminated oesophagus, *I* fall against its wall, *I* find m/yself propelled from one point to another to the level of the arterial arch, *I* am utterly shattered by its throbbing, *I* am driven to the level of the auricles and the ventricles of your heart only the membranes of the two walls separating m/e from them.

You are the tallest, Ishtar goddess of goddesses you are the powerful one, blessed be your name over centuries of centuries. You are the possessor of all power, you are strong impassive while you abide in the green in the violet of the heavens while they all await you, head erect you shine in the black nights, you are blinding in the days of summer, desire for you overwhelms m/e once for all together with terror as befits all your adorers, the earth the trees the waters the rivers the torrents the seas the stars of the sky do they not tremble at the mere utterance the mere vibration of your formidable name, Oh that *I* might be dumb or m/y tongue fall out when *I* seek your black shining visage your gilded limbs your vigorous knees, foolish *I* am if *I* complain aloud of the glorious supremely divine Astarte she who has no beginning who has no end she who is, she who cannot have been that which she will not be. Ishtar Astarte m/y beloved eternal one *I* invoke you *I* implore you, *I* thirst for your benevolent tears as much as your rage and your ferocity, not one has prayed to you without your hearing her voice you who have created all woman to be loved by you, m/y adorable one appear once more tonight that *I* may lay m/yself down beside you that m/y hands may touch you that m/y perfumes may please you, *I* shall speak or else not say a word as you wish, *I* shall sing or else stay waiting for your voice to issue from your mouth m/y solestial one m/y celestial one m/y sovereign mistress, blessed be thy name.

Your hair stiffened by the frost sparkles. Your hands are stilled against your upturned throat. The green and blue dawn makes a light travel over your naked unfolded body. Your eyes are not closed, they do not see. The women bearing torches kneel beside you, your face is lit by the gleams. Shadows pass over your teeth, in your mouth *I* see your palate. One of the women begins slowly to massage your breast back loins belly with her strong hands. Another wraps you in sheepskins. Someone heats water on a fire in the snow. The boiling water put into the bottles warms your petrified body at the places they touch. *I* am paralysed, *I* am afraid. *I* begin to embrace you as warmly as is in m/y power. *I* pass m/y breath into your mouth hoping to reach your lungs. Now *I* am naked, *I* lie down on top of you, *I* roll on your body to give you the warmth of m/y blood of m/y muscles. Here and there you soften. It is the muscles of one of your arms. It is the hollow of one of your shoulders, it is your throat, it is your wrists and your palms. You are seized by a trembling that *I* barely perceive. *I* cry out with all m/y might. The torches sway in the hands of the bearers bent over you. Now a rattle issues from your mouth, *I* receive it on m/y lips, *I* wait for you to pronounce m/y name. In m/y impatience *I* begin to dig in the snow with bare hands, *I* look for snowdrops and black hellebore to place on you. You strive to raise your head, you move your hands, you look around you, you ask to drink. The sea around the island is frozen.

I have discovered on your arms on your shoulders at the top of your back on your loins on your chest violet marks ranged on the skin of your body. You, you do not conceal them, you do not place your hands palms open over the affected places indicating that one of the women has laid claim to you. You stand opposite m/e every muscle tense a smile irradiating from your mouth over your entire face as you look at m/e. M/y fingers touch the ridges one after the other, a swelling magnifying the points of contact as *I* perceive them. *I* feel a pain spreading from m/y fingertips to m/y wrists extending the length of m/y arms as far as m/y throat making m/y chest burst. It is at that moment that *I* spit a part of m/y right lung a soft bland mass to the back of m/y throat and palate. *I* take it between m/y fingers, *I* pull, *I* wrench it out, *I* hold it pale pink still living before your eyes, *I* shake it, *I* squeeze it, *I* crush it on your skin against the pearl-shaped weals ranged one beside the other. M/y left lung comes in its turn into m/y mouth, in fragments, its bulk chokes m/e in passage its elastic substance touching m/y teeth, *I* bite it, *I* chew it, *I* swallow it, *I* spit it out, *I* spread it from the edge of m/y lips over the entire surface of m/y body. You are seized with convulsions, *I* persist. *I* spread the pink paste over the inward of your arms. There is no smile on your face but the puckering that

95

precedes tears. *I* forbid you to weep. Untiringly *I* anoint you with m/y living cement, *I* cradle you in m/y arms, *I* carry you, *I* press m/y lips to your lips m/y tongue forcing you to open your mouth, *I* insert into you the last pulverized vestiges of m/y lungs which you swallow shrinking which you prepare to digest or to vomit whose intromission you are unable to refuse their evacuation from m/y body being effected with the greatest violence by the rending open of m/y chest m/y eyes fixed untiringly on the long violet marks which reappear beneath the bruises their sight tearing the most desperate cries from m/e m/y cruellest one that have ever issued from m/e.

The temperature of the island cools. A sudden tornado sweeps the coast loosening the moorings of the boats in the ports. At sea-level the wind blows at a speed so great as to be unrecordable. There are a great many fisher-women at sea. You are among them. The first wave to overflow the beaches covers the houses and their occupants at a bound. Torn-out wooden stakes rise suddenly into the air. *I* see some swimmers energetically attempting to withstand the eddies. *I* see nothing more. Kneeling in

96

the garden up above m/y hands over m/y ears m/y hair
tossed *I* begin to pray to Sappho m/y all-powerful one
save her from dying. One after the other the tide-race
carries away the huts on the seashore where the nets dry.
If you must die m/y most adored one let the entire island
be delivered to destruction, let not one of us remain alive.
As for m/e *I* look out to sea again, *I* do not weep. *I* see
the boats empty of their occupants flung up one after the
other over the ruined dwelling-places. Then the first
rescues are organized. With ropes with cranes with boat-
hooks it is possible to evacuate the women coastguards
among whom few losses are to be deplored. Already the
bodies of the drowned are laid out on the terraces of the
upper town. Briskly the women mass in their hundreds,
songs whose beat is marked by the tom-toms aid the
quickest conduct of the operations. *I* do not find you. *I*
do not recognize among the wrecks your black boat
marked with the violet sign you affect. *I* move towards
the coral grotto where we often fall asleep from fatigue.
There away from the storm in an absolute calm with
none of the furious sounds of the wind with none of the
shouts or songs of mourning or songs of work you are
asleep in the bottom of the boat m/y triumphant one
smiling, the orange reflections of the coral are sped over
your naked body by the movement of the waves. So
Sappho the all-powerful has allowed you to reach the
grotto which has saved more than one woman in days of
tempest. *I* swim up to you in all haste. *I* let m/yself fall
at your side. *I* begin to sing in a very low voice glory to
Sappho over centuries of centuries so be it.

97

Your hand followed by your arm have entered into m/y throat, you traverse m/y larynx, you arrive at m/y lungs, you itemize m/y organs, you make m/e die ten thousand deaths while *I* smile, you rip out m/y stomach, you tear m/y intestines, you project the uttermost fury into m/y body, *I* cry out but not from pain, *I* am overtaken seized hold of, *I* go over to you entirely, *I* explode the small units of m/y ego, *I* am threatened, *I* am desired by you. A tree shoots in m/y body, it moves its branches with extreme violence with extreme gentleness, or else it is a bush of burning thorns it tears the other side of m/y exposed muscles m/y inside m/y interiors, *I* am inhabited, *I* am not dreaming, *I* am penetrated by you, now *I* must struggle against bursting to retain m/y overall perception, *I* reassemble you in all m/y organs, *I* burst, *I* reassemble you, sometimes your hand sometimes your mouth sometimes your shoulder sometimes your whole body, when m/y stomach is affected your stomach responds when m/y lungs rattle your lungs rattle, finally *I* am without depth without place m/y stomach appearing between m/y breasts m/y lungs traversing the skin of m/y back.

The three mares arrive abreast in broad daylight. On their flanks their coat is struck by sunlight. *I* look at the mauve or pale-green pools among the stretches of damp sand. You amidst them you advance sombrely, you shake your mane, you begin to neigh, you draw near, your yellow eyes fixed on m/e. Now the pace of the three unsaddled mares slows, their coats moistened by the sea glisten, the skin quivers over their muscles, there are no flies to stroke them only the wind and the insistent heat of the sun. Their legs bend with enormous slowness, *I* can see for a long time the curve at their knees, then they touch the ground again while another leg is lifted in its turn. Flank to flank you all advance, you yourself, mouth open not held by any bit teeth bared, you pant, your nostrils quiver. Coming up to m/e you kneel before the little girls like the mounts in painted pictures, your head bends and tosses, *I* place both m/y hands on your mane, *I* hold your head, *I* pass m/y tongue over your muzzle, *I* glide against your belly in order to mount you. Then you bridle, your coat grazes m/y vulva and m/y thighs, when *I* lie down m/y belly is pressed against your back. You set off at a gallop towards the sea, you whinny with all your might, the wind blows at m/y ears, it upholds m/y hair behind, m/y breasts judder, when *I* turn round *I* see the island dwellings all small and distant, then *I* begin to whinny in m/y turn as loudly as *I* can, *I* slide along your length, *I* let m/yself fall to the ground, now *I* gallop even though it means forcing the pace to keep up with you, m/y feet happily trample the sand, the sun on the sea scorches m/y eyes, we enter the sea head-on, whoever retraces their steps it will not be you nor *I* m/y dearest, your body steams, your nostrils flare, m/y flank touches your flank, coolness comes from the water, a dazzle comes to m/e from the sun and the sea, sound reaches m/e from the waves, a warm breath touches m/y neck yours.

Your hair is undone over your face. The hairs are taken one at a time and fixed to a hoop in a half-circle all around your head thus held away from your face by their whole length. So stretched they resound beneath m/y fingertips which slide along them. The infinitely soft fragile sound can be varied over the whole extent of the instrument. Your face is totally obscured by this obscure stiff veil. *I* regard you from below, your cheeks are very pale. Whenever m/y fingers make your hairs vibrate you begin to sigh. Now *I* follow them with some dexterity and faster and faster. The sound-waves create a pressure around us, a change occurs in the atmosphere, a slow movement commences, an eddy develops, a current becomes apparent. You drift off suddenly, you sway from side to side, you are uplifted. Your hands cling to m/y hair, now you rise up, you drag m/e carried by m/y hair. You start to spin on yourself, *I* copy your

THE DORSALS THE ILIACS THE
TERES THE QUADRATI THE TRI-
ANGULAR THE PYRAMIDALS THE
ABDOMINALS THE GLUTEALS THE
BICEPS THE TRICEPS THE TENDONS
OF ACHILLEA THE SUPINATORS
THE TIBIALS THE SUBLIMI THE
ABDUCTORS OF THE EYE THE
RECTI SUPERIORES THE COM-
PLEXES THE DIAPHRAGM THE
VAGINA THE ANUS THE SOFT
PALATE THE CONNECTIVE TISSUE
THE MENINGES THE DURA MATER
THE ARACHNOID THE PIA MATER
THE SCLERA THE CORNEA THE
RETINA THE CHOROID THE GUMS
THE PLEURA THE PERITONEUM
THE OMENTUM

movement, *I* effect the same slow rotation m/y hands
seeking points of support. It is not then possible to arrest
the movement it is so slow. An irresistible force emanates
from you and sweeps m/e away. *I* close m/y eyes. *I* let
m/yself go. M/y fingers grope for your hairs which they
touch and cause to resonate. A very audible music now
makes itself heard. At the same time you sing. The sounds
rise spread grow louder. The movement with which you
spin as you bear m/e away grows faster. Now we are
spinning rapidly at the top of the palm-trees and suddenly m/y most ravishing one you begin to laugh while
you draw m/e in a straight line above the island dwellings towards the sea.

M/y vile one *I* recall the summer sky traversed by heat
haze in the black night where you have confined m/e.
M/y eyes are covered, m/y ears are stopped, m/y throat
is gagged to my lips' edge, m/y armpits are filled, m/y
navel is knotted, m/y vagina is packed from m/y uterus
to m/y labia, m/y colon is blocked to m/y anus. *I* recall
the clouds of dust, *I* still have in mind the reflections of

the sun on the leaves of the trees, *I* recall a river, *I* recall
the wild races in the hot hay-covered meadows m/y most
atrocious one in the immobility you impose on m/e. At
m/y groins in m/y iliac arteries the needles introduce the
fluid which paralyses m/e, m/y kidneys are fit to burst,
they press on m/y overheated intestines, in m/y throat
the fluid introduced into m/y carotids spreads to m/y
brain, it blows all m/y circuits, m/y tongue chokes m/e
striving to emerge from m/y mouth. *I* recall the soft
contact of breasts and bellies the slow sinuous comings
and goings the warmth of the skins the delicacy of touching in the gehenna to which you have condemned m/e
m/y tormentor without entrails all reassembled on m/e
horribly confined exploding into a thousand impotent
fragments to disjoin m/e completely.

A great tumult on the circle awakens m/e. Already you
return with the news. The first women to awaken have
announced the pure and simple disappearance of the
vowels. Consternation reigns. Numerous lamentations
are heard. You must write down the news for m/e if *I*
am to understand its meaning. Your lip your tongue
modulate the new language in guttural sounds, the

uttered consonants jostled one against the other produce gruntings gratings scrapings of the vocal cords, your voice untried in this pronunciation speeds up or slows down and yet you cannot stop talking. The novel effect of the movement of your cheeks and mouth the difficulty the sounds have in making their way out of your mouth are so comical that *I* choke with laughter, *I* fall over backwards, m/y tears stream, *I* regard you still and silent, *I* am increasingly overcome by laughter, suddenly you too are affected, you burst out, your cheeks colour, you fall over backwards as the women's clamour is heard outside their interpellations the long incomprehensible phrases pronounced by one of them and repeated interminably by many others. A new arrival makes heard at regular intervals the lugubrious sound of a tom-tom which she beats to a funereal rhythm. The unwonted resonances of the now transformed language repeated by more and more voices produce uncontrollable waves movements of air masses of clouds. A heavy rumbling is heard, lightning flashes follow each other blindingly, the storm breaks with such a din as at once to cover the sound of the thousands of voices. Now the women flee along the sandy island paths seeking the shelter of the open pavilions. The rain has begun to patter. The tom-tom is being beaten vigorously somewhere in the distance this time to a rapid rhythm. Their voices join in song. The smell of the wet leaves and the grass in the gardens comes to m/e overwhelmingly, you stand opposite m/e, *I* see you are crying and laughing at the same time heifer suckling-lamb m/y best-beloved may grief abandon you for ever.

I leave you alone in the room where you have spoken to m/e as to a stranger where you have not recognized m/e despite the glare of the lanterns. At m/y order the women prepare m/y severed limbs m/y arms m/y thighs m/y legs whose flesh is meticulously removed and boiled for a long time, they offer it to you surrounded by different sauces on glittering plates each plate bearing a different name to please you. You consume them readily their appellations do not strike you with astonishment. Bringing you a finger-bowl and crystallized fruits the women inform you of what and of whom you have eaten. Immediately you begin to vomit, a profuse perspiration appears on your cheeks on your temples without your shedding a tear, you fall flat on your face your stomach utterly revolted hiccups preventing you from resuming breathing, the women support you beneath the arms, they speak to you at length whispering enumerating each of the parts you have eaten while without begging for mercy you empty yourself completely the nutriment now replaced by long green spurts of bile then by splashes of blood your tongue outside your mouth, you choke, you spit m/e out, you vomit m/e up, you lose all your colour, momentarily you faint crying that *I* am accursed, when your consciousness and memory return you reject m/e anew with violence without interruption.

The two black boats approach each other bearing an identical violet sign. The water of the sea is flat. It holds a blue and golden light. When the one and the other boat are side by side you draw yourself up to your full height turned towards m/e. Without a signal the combat begins, arms seeking arms, shoulders touching shoulders, legs thighs pressed against the sides of the boats, bare feet scrape the wood essaying rapid movements to straddle both boats at once. *I* see that deep down sharks shadow the sea coming and going incessantly. Suddenly *I* am afraid, *I* attempt to repel you, *I* press with the flat of m/y hands on the side of m/y boat, *I* push on yours, *I* try to separate them, *I* double up with the exertion. Then you, you strike a blow on the back of m/y neck with the edge of your hand. *I* strive to stand up, you press with both palms on m/y bare back, so raising yourself up you arch your back, you let yourself glide behind m/e to the bottom of m/y boat. *I* start to tremble, m/y hair stands on end while both m/y hands are grasped by your hands behind m/y loins. You encircle m/e with one of your arms, you lift m/e up. One of m/y legs comes in contact with the water, it is brutally torn off by the open mouth of one of the sharks. M/y other leg is bent at a right angle. Well-braced against the side of m/y boat you throw m/e down, you cast both m/y arms to the sharks which devour them dragging m/e down, later m/y head is torn off, m/y eyes momentarily turned upwards in m/y head as it falls see cruellest of all monsters the beautiful movement you employ to throw m/y mutilated trunk m/y pelvis as far as possible.

Cursed be the frenzy which grips m/e on hearing your voice all naked detached from your body far from your throat that emits it. Enough to burst the vessels of m/y temples behind m/y eyes at the surface of the auricles of m/y heart, the sound-wave reaches m/e. It affects m/y ears the hammer-bones violently strike the anvils the semicircular canals the cochleas begin to whirl, m/y entire brain reels, m/y throat contracts, m/y eyes subjected to an enormous pressure begin to flow, m/y tongue issues from m/y mouth. M/y lungs expelling all their contained air retract at an insane speed. Your voice invades m/e further still, it descends like a tendril to the bottom of m/y stomach, it traverses the duodenum, it follows every convolution of m/y intestines, it hunts m/e down, it batters from within against all m/y parietes, *I* am crammed to bursting in all m/y hollow places, *I* am finally cut to pieces, m/y arms m/y legs dangle, as the pressure mounts they eventually fall off. Darkness falls in the orbits of m/y eyes on m/y eardrums in m/y larynx. M/y neck involved bends and separates from m/y trunk, m/y entire body separated into its parts directs black stomach black intestines black heart vulva green bile into the black darkness inhabited only by your voice, that hateful voice m/y dearest one pursuing m/e tracking m/e down losing m/e undoing m/e finishing m/e off.

Perforations occur in your body and in m/y body joined together, our homologously linked muscles separate, the first current of air that infiltrates into the breach spreads at a crazy speed, creating a squall within you and within m/e simultaneously. You shake m/e and *I* do the same to you. Your teeth clash against m/y teeth. A wheezing issues from your mouth and maybe from m/y own. You sway from side to side and so do *I*. *I* perceive all the various winds assailing us. The orifices multiply over our two bodies causing m/y skin and your skin to burst alike. They are prolonged by tunnels whence the blood does not spurt. The wind enters everywhere, in every hole. *I* feel it passing from your stomach into m/ine, it has a passage at the level of the openings in our two throats, it is engulfed in the galleries created in our joined shoulders, it glides into the crevices of the muscles of our joined arms. It becomes so violent that it precipitates us one against the other, it brings us down, it flattens us. Under its pressure there is nothing else to do but to attempt to insinuate ourselves one into the other. Your eyes shine. Your hair tosses, it flails against your cheeks, it catches m/e on the forehead. The openings are now innumerable in the abdomens in your chest and mine along our intertwined limbs, they are to be seen every-where, everywhere the same wind traverses you traverses m/e. M/y fingers sink into the orifices in your back your loins, your fingers are inserted into the holes in m/y neck m/y cranium. In the end a tempest arrives, it rushes right through us, scattering the muscles. First *I* hear your cries, then *I* hear m/yself cry out as you do, there is a bellowing of sirens, they reverberate within the gaping tunnels on either side of our two bodies which now con-stitute a single organism pervaded by vibrations quiver-ing full of its own currents, is it not so m/y dearest?

Terror grips m/e to see you so pitiless and so serene. *I* draw near you, you do not look at m/e, *I* address you you do not answer m/e, *I* make gestures of allegiance you ignore them turned stolidly towards the field of pumpkins whose number you examine, fear descends to the hollows of m/y knees, *I* can hardly stand, *I* sigh very loudly, the greatest cold reaches m/e between m/y shoulderblades at m/y loins in m/y plexus. *I* begin to groan, *I* complain in a strident voice, *I* utter all the words *I* know. You indifferent you move along the paths of the kitchen-garden. Already the notebook you hold at eye-level is covered with signs. *I* begin to dance very clumsily with the jerky movements of a puppet, you do not see m/e. *I* sing a song which is known to you, *I* throw m/yself flat on m/y face in your path, you step over m/e and continue your gaze fixed only on the vegetables which trail on the ground. *I* speak to you of m/y long march of m/y unbroken zeal, you do not listen to m/e, only the field at your feet exacts your attention. From time to time you brush off a fly which alights on your cheek. At this moment which *I* take as a signal *I* respond with the gesture of reconciliation, you take no notice, you saunter along the avenues unhurriedly gliding on your feet. At a given moment *I* let m/yself fall on a cluster of pump-kins which strike m/y stomach violently hiding them from your sight. Then *I* tear them up very quickly, *I* pull at the stalks, *I* throw them as far as *I* can crawling over the vegetables while swallowing one immediately vomited whole crushing them between m/y powerful palms causing them to burst as water-spray and pips, then *I* run upright, *I* trample them all under your eyes, *I* come and go ardently destroying the entire crop that you have requisitioned for the island. Then you look at m/e, then you curse m/e, you invoke against m/e infernal Persephone the triple goddess, your knees your fists batter m/e, there is an explosion at m/y temples, your hate-filled words hiss in m/y ears, *I* see your eyes and m/y knees m/y most intractable one buckle finally before you.

Against your ankles deeply embedded in the ground there occurs a movement, particles separate, small stones are loosened. The first snake to coil itself round one of your ankles is black glistening bearing orange bands. It twines, it circles, it thrusts its fork-tongued mouth against your calf, it gains the bend of your knee and there supports itself, it winds around your knee, it reaches your thigh where it touches the internal muscles and the adductors on the inner side. The debris accumulates at the base of your legs. Your other leg is seized covered with rings ligated. Hundreds of apertures now lead to within the shifting ground. Three snakes, then eleven then scores crawl out. All are black and bear orange bands. They promptly advance their mouths over the ground which they barely touch. Their writhings bring them against your legs. They enlace you. At a given moment they cover you all over. Some dangle slackly from your immobilized forearms. Others descend on your trunk, glide between your breasts. Some wind between your shoulderblades. One of them is wound right round your neck. Another seeks to touch your eyes covered by your hair. At the first contact a shudder spreads over the surface of your skin to your entire body, your hair-follicles erect and the tips of your breasts. Your skin registers another series of reactions a barely perceptible watery ooze above your lips at the bends of your elbows and your knees then a streaming perspiration a shower of sweat soaking your hair your armpits and your pubic fleece trickling down your legs over the mass of snakes dropping to your feet moistening the shifted earth. Finally green violet red stains appear in patches, your throat is stained at the carotid, your skin flakes at a growing number of places. The snakes have finally concealed every part of your body. Then in your turn you begin slowly to coil and uncoil m/y most foul one sinuous black orange.

I walk over the black earth. It is strewn with cherry blossom. *I* look at the black and humid earth touched by m/y bare feet. *I* am halted by contact with something soft. Under the soles of m/y feet *I* see your eyeballs there, *I* have embedded them somewhat. Deprived of eyelids you gaze at m/e in the mounds of earth, your eyes gaze at m/e, *I* start back, *I* bend down, *I* throw m/yself flat on m/y face to gather them in the hollow of m/y hands. It is your closed lips thrown a little further off that m/y hands touch. Your whole body is in fragments here, *I* pick up your hair in handfuls, your nose is at some distance, your face is all dispersed. *I* begin to cry out with all m/y might, *I* crawl along the ground m/y hair on end. *I* recognize one of your arms then the other. *I* find your two breasts your severed throat, *I* touch your outspread hands, your thighs are here, your knees your legs all intact. *I* collapse over your belly, tears of blood flow over m/y cheeks, *I* call to you in a strident voice, m/y heart makes m/e feel like death leaping into m/y mouth. *I* perceive your ears. *I* cover them with kisses. Your body is spread still warm bleeding over the entire surface of the ploughed field. *I* gather you up piece by piece. *I* reassemble you. *I* lick each of your parts sullied by the earth. *I* speak to you. *I* am seized by vomiting, *I* choke, *I* shriek, *I* speak to you, *I* yearn for you with such

113

marvellous strength that all of a sudden the pieces fall together, you don't have a finger or a fragment missing. Then *I* begin to breathe into your half-open mouth into your nose your ears your vulva, *I* breathe without ceasing lying here on you naked in the black earth. Cherry-blossom falls on you, *I* brush it aside.

Sappho when *I* beseech her causes a violet lilac-smelling rain to fall over the island. *I* do not seek the shelter of the trees under pretext of escaping the moisture or to contemplate the divers signs multiplying between earth and sky. *I* stand head erect, mouth open, *I* thank Sappho the very tender goddess while you m/y very radiant one hold m/y hands. The clouds are hardly any darker than the water dripping from them, the sun lights them transparently, the hills are their exact replica the other way round violet rounded, the olive-trees seem paler by contrast more silver than green. You release m/y hands to undo my girdle, you remove m/y clothes, *I* watch you doing this, you too are naked, your skin is white in the

THE CORPORI CAVERNOSA THE
VAGINAL BULBS THE SKELETON
THE VERTEBRAL COLUMN THE
CLAVICLES THE RIBS THE
STERNUM THE HUMERI THE RADII
THE ULNAE THE CARPALS THE
METACARPALS THE PHALANGES
THE ILIAC BONES THE PELVIS THE
SACRUM THE COCCYX THE
FEMORA THE PATELLAE THE
FIBULAE THE TIBIAE THE TARSALS
THE METATARSALS THE CRURALS
THE MASTOIDS THE ORBITS THE
PATELLAE THE MONS PUBIS THE
VULVA THE WOMB THE BLADDER
THE INTESTINES THE KIDNEYS
THE SPLEEN THE LIVER THE GALL-
BLADDER THE STOMACH THE
LUNGS THE HEART

violet light, your lips are mauve, the chestnut of your eyes is mauve your hair is brown mauve, you raise your arms, you begin to stir singing, you whistle between your teeth, you sing, loudly *I* praise Sappho the all-attentive, you recapitulate m/y phrases in your song, you spin them out, you modulate them interminably, you rotate on yourself, the water strikes your cheeks your shoulders your breasts your belly your back your buttocks your thighs your calves, violet rings appear on your skin, they enlarge progressively, immense circles cover your entire body, m/y fingers touch them while you laugh, you lift your feet so that their soles may be stained in their turn, you fall backwards on the sand all violet, the inward of your arms and thighs is involved, *I* inhale you m/y very odoriferous one, you smell very headily of lilac, Sappho could have done no better by clasping you against her violet breasts, now *I* lick you, you roll over and over, thousands of grains of violet sand sting your body, you are aglow with all your fires, your hair your pubic fleece that of your armpits is definitively violet and when as they say *I* look deep into your violet eyes m/y adored one *I* do not recognize them, you take hold of m/y fingers so they may touch your body so *I* may familiarize m/yself with your new appearance so *I* may interpret you m/y most mauve one, glory to Sappho over centuries of centuries.

You are among the lavender pickers. The sun is already high over the plateau. *I* see the rectilinear movement of your file over the red dry earth. The brims of the straw hats do not flap in the wind. No bird cries. The sea is visible right in front of you a uniform blue paled by the light at the foot of the highest cliff of the island. *I* have abandoned the lookout for the fishing-boats whose arrival *I* ought to announce with blasts of the conch. M/y empty place at the end of the mole can be seen from everywhere. *I* progress in a series of leaps, oftenest *I* lie flat on m/y face at the edge of the field. *I* cannot distinguish your silhouette from the place *I* occupy. When at last it is discernible, one of the women signals a rest pause. One after the other they let the large jute sacks fall to the ground. You, you remain standing turning your back to m/e regarding the sea straight in front of you. At a given moment you bring to your mouth the gourd fastened to your belt and drink slowly. A woman begins to sing in a very loud voice squatting on her heels. Another takes her flute to accompany the voice. The smell of the lavender is heady, there is a great movement of bees wasps hornets butterflies. *I* have to stay quiet hidden. Presently when your column advances towards the sea *I* shall endeavour to approach you from behind calling to you and making you come to m/e without the others taking m/e by surprise. *I* regard your back the nape of your neck your hair. *I* experience a wish to see your eyes. Then you turn round, you look across to where *I* am, you march with great strides, you move towards m/e, now you are running, *I* hear you call out, you are above m/e, you dominate m/e with your full stature, you laugh, you fall on m/e before *I* have time to speak, your hair trails over m/y eyes, the sky *I* see through it quivers, *I* feel you striking m/y ribs, you ask in a hissing voice if *I* wish to be expelled from this land blessed above all others because of m/y very great folly, you condemn m/e to every hell, you spit in m/y eyes, you ask m/e how many times it will be necessary to depart once more to travel to find a place to live, you ask m/e if *I* wish to die and at the moment *I* say yes your strong hand falls on m/e, darkness covers m/y eyes, *I* feel the cold spreading up m/y thighs.

M/y fingers are spread out nailed down, m/y palms are turned towards the sun, the metacarpals the phalanges are extended. M/y hands are like stars. *I* see at m/y wrists the blue veins, a broad network on the inside of m/y arms. You apply your new procedure to m/e to inoculate the sun, the veins and arteries of m/y wrists artificially dilated. You are obliged to hold m/e on the ground because of the shaking of m/y body. The tips of your fingers are sheathed in supple mirrors. They radiate they catch the heat they irradiate they burn. M/y veins and arteries affected gradually catch fire. A subtle warmth reaches m/y palms m/y arms m/y elbows under m/y armpits. M/y heart ventricles and auricles suddenly begin to explode. Your lips are applied firmly to m/y throat. The heat becomes explosive. Colours violet orange red pervade m/y entire body, m/y eyes are caught in the overthrow the fall of intense colouration, they fall they fall, *I* receive them on m/y belly. M/y ears lips tongue abandon m/e in their turn, they bound here and there on m/y breasts and m/y thighs. You diffuse the sun's fire over m/e, you impose it on m/e without pause, dispersed throughout the circuits of m/y blood it fastens on m/y liver m/y lungs m/y spleen. A smell of burnt flesh rises, now you hold m/e round the waist, the roasting reaches you, a smoke-screen forms before your eyes, the muscles splutter disappearing around our cheeks. At last our blackened skulls clash together, at last boneless with black holes to see you with without hands to touch you *I* am you you are m/e irreversibly m/y best-beloved.

Your limbs gathered under you you progress in m/y direction, your belly is flush with the ground, your ears are turned back over your head, a growling issues from your mouth while you advance slowly halting at every stage to take cover surveying m/e from ambush your chin resting on your forepaws. Your fur is grey streaked with polar blue save on the belly where it is a golden beige, it ensheathes your neck your skull all round your cheeks, only your female face is exposed your forehead nose eyes cheeks chin lips. At times you leap with your feline bound to reach m/e with your paws seizing m/e by the neck, I struggle, I make you roll on m/e m/y mouth seeking your mouth. You are the same size as all the others. But you progress doubled up in kangaroo fashion. I am seized with a kind of frivolity. I make extravagant bounds which distance m/e from you, they are not the gambols of kids but precise calculated leaps which might equally bring m/e near to you, I enjoy m/y springiness. And then I find it pleasurable when I touch m/y fur with m/y mouth, then I make m/y way towards you, I begin to nibble the hairs of your neck of your loins your belly your back. I learn with you the game cats play when they roll up into a ball when they curl up on themselves when they prepare to pounce on each other. The possible combinations are very many. A smile uncovers your teeth when you leap on m/y back taking m/e by surprise your claws immediately gripping m/e unbalancing m/e. At a given moment *I* go with you to bathe. M/y fur impregnated with water weighs m/e down. *I* cling to you until your grey hairs drip with water in their turn. Only your face is dry and sleek, m/y lips and tongue touch it as *I* take you in m/y arms.

I begin with the tips of your fingers, *I* chew the phalanges *I* crunch the metacarpals the carpals, *I* slaver at your wrists, *I* disarticulate the ulnae with great delicacy, *I* exert pressure on the trochlea, *I* tear away the biceps from the humerus, *I* devour it, *I* eat m/y fill of you m/y so delectable one, m/y jaws snap, *I* swallow you, *I* gulp you down. Separated from the acromion both your arms are detached from your shoulders. You sovereign radiant you regard m/e. M/y saliva spreads over your breasts, long fragments of flesh separate from the muscles falling over your neck staining your white throat, carefully *I* take them between m/y teeth, *I* chew them voraciously, then *I* look at you and *I* am overwhelmed with great pity to see you so mutilated deprived of both your arms your bust bloodied. The food you are weighs on m/e within m/y stomach, *I* am suddenly revolted, *I* vomit you up, a great liquid half-digested stinking steaming mass falls on your belly. You become very pale at this point you throw yourself back with a great cry, tears spurt strongly from your eyes spattering m/e, you say it is unbearable to see m/e vomit you up, *I* am overcome by greater pity than ever, *I* begin to eat you again as fast as *I* can m/y so adored one *I* lick the last scraps on your belly, *I* get rid of the traces of blood, *I* absorb you m/y very precious one, *I* retain you within m/e.

I am at the Golgotha you have all abandoned. You sleep among the women a paper tigress, you sleep one arm folded over your head your hair wildly disposed around your face, you resemble one of the Gorgons terrible powerful ruddy in dream. During this period deprived of the aid of your strength *I* lie face to the ground, fear grips m/e and the desire to go on living with you in this garden, not one of you knows anything

of m/y anguish, then *I* implore the great goddess m/y
mother and *I* say to her mother mother why have you
forsaken m/e, she remains silent while you sleep, not a
breath of wind stirs m/y hair, *I* cry out in m/y distress
mother mother why have you forsaken m/e, someone
turns over groaning in her sleep, *I* move crawling toward
the top of the garden, *I* leave you m/y dearest, hardly
have *I* left the place where you lie than *I* can no longer
perceive you in the expanse of sleeping bodies, now *I*
shriek fit to burst m/y lungs, not one of you awakens, yet
m/y voice issues so powerfully from m/y throat that it
injures m/e in passage, *I* do not recognize it, a red mist
comes before m/y eyes, a bloody sweat traverses m/y
pores, suddenly it covers m/e entirely, m/y very tears
dripping in great drops on m/y arms stain them with
blood, bloody m/y saliva falling in strings from m/y
mouth, red the moon when she appears in the sky red the
earth red the night *I* see all red around m/e, *I* cry out
in m/y great distress mother mother why have you forsaken m/e, *I* hear nothing but the continued stridulations
of the crickets, the low close-packed crowns of the olive-
trees do not separate to make way for her coming to m/e
bare-footed her black hair and garments visible between
the pale leaves, *I* turn towards you but you are all
asleep.

I swim far out to sea that here bears thousands of seaweeds to look for you. *I* am totally enveloped in the black liquid mass, m/y body is rolled by the water rolled up in the vegetation. No moon, no stars are visible. *I* have lost sight of the island shores, *I* do not perceive the fisher-women's boats drawn up with their flickering lights. The warm changing waves cradle m/e bear m/e away. Some-times a fish comes alongside brushes against m/e, only its motion is perceptible, *I* cannot estimate its size. The sound of the sea boomings rumblings rattlings impacts clashings surgings enters m/y ears making m/y eardrums vibrate, a pain arises there, reverberates within m/y brain. *I* seek you in the dark of the sea and the dark of the night which *I* cannot distinguish, *I* emerge from the water, m/y head shoulders torso lifted as far as m/y waist pushing down on the water with m/y legs and m/y arms straining m/y loins to look as far as possible. You are nowhere in this mass your white body spread on the surface of the water your shoulders your back lying there your hair dragging behind your eyes closed. Great sea-weeds cling to m/y neck m/y shoulderblades m/y waist m/y pubis m/y thighs. *I* shout your name whenever *I* am not made breathless by exertion. *I* do not hear your voice answering m/e. The sea murmurs. There are no bird-calls at this time. *I* am seized with hoarseness which prevents m/y voice issuing from m/y throat. M/y muscles stiffened by fatigue eventually immobilize m/e. Then *I* submit to the power of the waves. The water enters by m/y mouth by m/y lungs, *I* cannot spit it all out again, as the pressure grows m/y intestines m/y stomach are invaded, m/y parietes burst, the skin of m/y belly splits apart, the water enters and leaves m/e. An obscurity develops the night of m/y body redoubling the other, suddenly it seems to m/e that you are the water which comes and goes in the closest confines of m/y body m/y very glorious one m/y most eternal beloved, it seems that you are that which engulfs m/e now and for ever without m/y desiring any of all you others to implore the goddesses for m/e.

Abominable mistress *I* am bled dry by you. Buzzings affect m/y ears the sound of your intermittent gasping respiration the sound of your frenetic voice, still from time to time *I* seem to hear your laughter. You shall not wring from m/e the cries of a sow whose throat is being slit. Besides it is too late. M/y arteries have been severed, my veins systematically dilated. The plantar peroneal tibial femoral iliac carotid ulnar radial arteries are most rudely severed, slashed is the better word. M/y saphenous femoral iliac axilliary basilic cephalic radial jugular veins are kept open by glass pipettes inserted therein. *I* do not hear m/y blood running away. M/y heart is squeezed sponged, it bounds intermittently or else it suddenly comes to a halt, it goes by fits and starts. M/y blood quits m/y brain, it is leached from my face by m/y temporal arteries by m/y facial veins, m/y cheeks are hollowed, m/y blood leaves m/y attached limbs m/y arms legs groins, it does not flow through m/y intestines, *I* am no longer nourished, m/y lungs are not oxygenated, m/y breathing is increasingly more difficult. *I* see how completely emptied with no more thickness than a geographical map m/y skin is going to be stretched out taut by you m/y organs all flat falling spontaneously m/y bones turned into powder crumbling, m/y entire body now absolutely ready to be fastened with drawing-pins on your wall, may you be accursed once and for all you whom *I* clearly see standing sometimes passing your fingers over m/y flattened body seeking the traces of former canals of former orifices.

I wrench out your teeth one by one, your minuscule short and square incisors your well-developed pointed canines your premolars *I* arrange them in front of m/e, one by one *I* see them gleaming, they are removed with their roots, to whom should *I* offer them if not to Sappho the most distant telling her that reassembled they constitute the most living necklace ever to be seen by female eyes. *I* ask you which of us shall wear it, you part your lips m/y mutilated one over your bloodstained gums, *I* insert m/y tongue into each socket in succession, *I* probe your wounds, m/y lips m/y fingers receive your blood, with m/y mouth with m/y hands *I* make red marks and traces on your body, your mouth bleeds without stopping, you do not complain m/y so silent one, you regard m/e fixedly while in great haste *I* cover your body with great signs, while *I* am all gooseflesh, while *I* seize the small shreds of your ripped flesh between m/y intact teeth, while you smile horribly at m/e you most beautiful of all women.

THE OESOPHAGUS THE BRAIN THE
CIRCULATION THE RESPIRATION
THE NUTRITION THE ELIMINA-
TION THE DEFAECATION THE RE-
PRODUCTION [XX + XX = XX] THE
REACTIONS PLEASURE EMOTION
VISION SMELL TASTE TOUCH
HEARING THE VOCAL CORDS THE
CRIES THE WAILINGS THE
MURMURS THE HOARSENESS THE
SOBS THE SHRIEKS THE VOCIFERA-
TIONS THE WORDS THE SILENCES
THE WHISPERINGS THE MODULA-
TIONS THE SONGS THE
STRIDENCIES THE LAUGHS THE
VOCAL OUTBURSTS THE LOCO-
MOTION

The women carry m/e by force to the theatre in the middle of the garden. *I* struggle. More than one strikes m/e and holds m/e still. There they lay m/e on the ground limbs tied together a gag in m/y mouth compelling m/e to look. Your entire body is fixed petrified in an iridescent block of plastic. *I* see your wide-open eyes, *I* see your smiling mouth, *I* see your hair floating as when you run, *I* see your arms spread on either side of you your legs halted in mid-stride, *I* see your belly, *I* see your sex, *I* see your shoulders, *I* see your breasts. The sun makes the whole block shine, your cheeks sparkle, your eyes are dazzling. Then *I* faint away. The women compel m/e to go on looking at you making m/e regain consciousness. *I* try with all m/y might to cry out. The gag chokes m/e, *I* struggle, *I* tug at m/y bonds, *I* weep with great sobs, *I* look at you in your full height you loom over m/e, m/e cast at your feet, *I* look at you and *I* see that you look at m/e too, m/y heart jolts, something explodes in m/y chest, so you are alive there completely imprisoned in that matrix by what means goddesses, you are alive, you look at m/e day of horror and joy, *I* struggle even as they finally untie m/e, *I* rush towards you, *I* embrace you, *I* speak to you, you do not stir, you look at m/e, *I* see your eyes close enough to touch you. *I* turn round towards the women grouped at the foot of the statue, *I* clasp their knees, *I* implore them very loudly weeping to place m/e with you there inside that matrix.

I am she who holds the secret of your name. *I* retain its syllables behind m/y closed mouth even while *I* would rather cry them out over the sea so that they might fall and be sombrely engulfed therein. The pitching of the boat displaces the violet image of the moon from here to there to one or other side of its axis. *I* sit up again, *I* regard the sky, *I* implore you. *I* can no longer bear alone the burden of the name which designates you m/y very beautiful one your neck your cheeks your gaze your glance your shoulders your breasts your arms your belly your sex your back your buttocks your thighs your legs your ankles your bare feet. You stand upright beside m/e on the deck your arms folded across your breast without speaking challenging m/e to break the silence brutally to impress on it the syllables of your accursed name. You smile your lips baring your teeth your head flung back now and again tossing your hair. You have no fear of m/e, you say, now while the sharks cruise incessantly in the deepest silence in the waters of the sea. Their violet bulks move rapidly returning to their point of departure making the boat the point of intersection of their comings and goings. At a given moment you illuminate them with a powerful lamp a luminous staff. Instantly they scatter, then they return describing ever-decreasing circles around the boat. You seize your submachine-gun, you

130

hold it straight before you aiming it at the bodies of the
sharks, you follow their movements the crackling of the
bullets making your forearms your arms your shoulders
shudder. Several of them are hit and collide in their
attempts to flee. The sea lit up by the lamp is stained
with their orange blood while they arrive in increasing
numbers crowding now beneath the boat creating such
eddies that it is in danger of capsizing you firing on them
teeth clenched a soft whistle issuing from your lips. *I*
begin to sing in a loud voice carried away by the combat
with extravagant gestures raising m/yself up and dropping down on to m/y heels then suddenly upright again
erect tense mouth open to shout your name once just
once m/y dearest one, you can permit it before what *I*
know must be the devouring of our bodies by the impatient creatures. It is then, changing your target divin-
ing what *I* am about to do, that you turn the barrel of
your weapon against m/e fierce silent casting m/e out
into the silence of the infinite spheres sole bearer of the
secret of your name alone with you m/y most unknown
now and for ever, so be it.

I have not the freedom of the city in the place where you live. The women have fashioned a dummy after m/y image. Now it burns on the vast square, *I* see it, the flames reach m/y feet, the smoke envelops m/e, through sulphur-coloured clouds *I* perceive the dense crowd, *I* hear the sorts of joyous songs which rise to their lips. They have bared their breasts as a sign of satisfaction. You are nowhere or else you are hiding overcome by distress and humiliation seeking the shade of the gardens and the sound of water on the terraces, or else you are under strict surveillance held in some place constrained to hear them in their song of death in which they tear m/e limb from limb. But it were better m/y so sensitive one that you were blind rather than watch wide-eyed what *I* endure at their behest. The flames have reached m/y naked belly m/y waist m/y breasts, blisters form where the skin burst with a disgusting sound. M/y buttocks m/y back held as far away as possible are involved in their turn enveloped in the flames the entire skin crackling fragmented, only m/y throat and face still emerge intact. The fire takes hold of m/y intestines, *I* writhe in slow sinusoidal movements, *I* rise up, *I* drop down, the fire perforates m/y chest shaking m/e right through, then *I* start to weep tears in sufficient quantity to extinguish several fires, *I* complain in a very loud voice in great revolt and anger against the wrong they do m/e beside you against the infamy the opprobrium with which they overwhelm m/e at a time when there are no longer any criminals, *I* cry out let them do it if they dare let them destroy m/e with such perfect meticulousness that no ashes of m/ine will remain on the earth or traces in the memory. But in the secret privacy of m/y body *I* hear a soft and furious growling, your name pervades and elates m/e, given that you m/y dearest one retain and harbour m/e within you *I* live for ever in the memory of the centuries, so be it.

The eye of your stomach is closed. *I* kiss its swarthy lid. The girdle of eyes that stretches from one hip to the other below your navel regards m/e whole. Drowsiness overtakes m/e. *I* shake m/y neck and head with all m/y might. *I* apply m/y mouth to the eyes of your belly. *I* make them roll under m/y lips one by one. They watch m/e, they all begin to shed tears together, *I* see them flow over your thighs and knees while you laugh with your single mouth, clasp m/e with your large hands. *I* am surrounded by the brilliance of your multiple eyes. A blue halo rises from the manifold whites. The eyes edging your pubis are closed. Each eye in the fold of

133

your elbow watches m/e. At your wrists the lids of the eyes which accompany the movements of your hands flutter. *I* seek your mouth with m/y mouth. *I* perceive the two eyes of your face, they watch m/e. Weakness overcomes m/e. Moving away from you *I* see that all the eyes of your body are fixed attentively on the different autonomous parts of m/y body in their actions in relation to one another. M/y muscles affected suddenly convulse. *I* see distinctly the gleam of your eyes ranged along the inside of your thighs, they stare at the skin of m/y belly close by. *I* see the winking of the ocular bracelets at your ankles. *I* see the two long rows which descend from your shoulders to the tip of your breasts. M/y entire body is riddled by your gaze. It immobilizes m/e. A mist comes before m/y eyes. Slackness takes m/e from the brain to the hollow of m/y loins, *I* am dizzy, *I* totter, *I* try to compel your eyes to a convergence, but at this point m/y all-seeing one you suddenly disintegrate m/e all your eyes fixed on m/e.

I have such a desire to weep that a pain catches the interior of m/y thorax m/y abdomen, the tears start from m/y eyes, they inundate you from above down with marvellous force, then *I* look at you, you are on the other side of this water, as soon as you near m/e m/y tears fall heavily on your feet making you start, they soak your hair your pubic hairs your armpits, your dampened skin changes its smell. *I* begin to hold you at arm's length, *I* compel you to move away from m/e. Your lips part over your well-squared teeth, then something provokes m/e to quit your person altogether as *I* see what you are engaged in doing, you file your teeth under your retracted lips, the dull whitish dust of the enamel issues from your mouth, you sharpen your teeth, you stop to look at m/e, all the white debris exhaled by you catches m/e in full face, hurriedly *I* open m/y eyes to look at you, you are still nearby, you smile incessantly with your pointed teeth, m/y tears flow anew, *I* weep with increasing ardour while your hands touch m/e, while you provoke m/e with your smiles and words to weep still more, but you know it you know it, *I* catch your sickness, you know it *I* am so sick from you that *I* am extremely happy.

You are present at the ceremony of the vulvas lost and found. Newly-arrived in the island you are unfamiliar with the ritual. *I* make you sit on the grass beside m/e,

I try to keep you informed m/y voice barely making itself heard amidst the sound of the drums the flutes the strident voices. The vulvas are represented by blue yellow green black violet red butterflies, their bodies are the clitorises, their wings are the labia, their fluttering represents the throbbing of the vulvas. Like you m/y refound one m/y dearest the butterflies return from a long journey. The brown and yellow Camberwell beauties the beautiful violet and pink parnassians the modest grey-yellow alucites the snowy bombyxes the giant orange blue ultramarine yellow pink violet uranias the blue arguses the peacocks with their large ocelli the swallow-tails splashed with black red blue the mauve orange violet green red admirals barely visible for a moment so rapid is their flight, the priestesses welcome them on the island shore. They wear violet dalmatics. They dance clapping their hands their bare feet touching the sand slowly rising and falling. The butterflies implored entreated not to make the fatal voyage across the sea return in clouds, they obscure the sun until dispersed over the gardens their separate colours become apparent. The priestesses wish them welcome and long life. The exhausted butterflies alight on the shoulders of the women present. Your arms are covered with them. Then m/y adored m/y most marvellous one *I* show you how to pick them up without spoiling their wings, *I* lick their bodies delicately to give them new strength. Five blue arguses poise on your spread fingers. The cries the laughter the songs make it difficult to hear you when you begin to sing in a very low voice.

They let their ears droop on their shoulders, you, you approach, you touch their lobes, then they move them against their cheeks their shoulders and further back against their hair and necks. You tease them, you nibble their ears, you lick them, you blow on them, with angelic patience they move the trunks of their mouths sucking you on the lips the cheeks and breasts addressing you, you do not understand them, you take m/e to task, *I* laugh, *I* see their gaze fixed centred on you, some of them are compelled to move their heads in order to see you for their pupils are immobile, when you start to leap around them they turn from side to side to follow your movements, you tug at their necklaces of teeth, your hands caress the fleece of their breasts which resembles that of your pubis. You rest your fingers on the butter-flies stuck to their shoulders, one of them has a small rat applied to her cheek, she takes your hand that you may caress it, as you flinch she makes you inducements with her mouth and its suctorial trunk, and *I, I* laugh leaning backwards because of this, irritated, you jostle m/e, you throw yourself on their group, you tug at their long-lobed ears with the greatest energy, some of them utter plaintive cries, they attempt to push you away without violence, but by dint of provoking them you obtain that which you desire and speak of in a very loud voice

inviting them to do it, it is possible that they have under-
stood since they suddenly fly away holding each other by
the hand in heavy flight flapping their ears at full speed
while you all excited call to them to wait for you, you
begin to run beneath them, *I* run to catch up with you,
they are just above our heads in a close rank, we run as
fast as they fly, we rival their speed our lungs ready to
burst with the exertion, they poise at a given moment
above the hill, *I* see that they are not at all out of breath,
we throw ourselves in their arms rolling on the ground,
they crush our wheezing chests against the soft tufted
hair of their breasts, their trunks nuzzle at our ears our
necks blow in our hair to spread it out, *I* smile m/y
marvellous one when you offer your very humid vulva
to their mouths. We cry out and laugh so loudly that the
other inhabitants of the island come running to join us.

I fall into a deep sleep, *I* fall into a well full of perfumes,
m/y lids are before m/y eyes, *I* fall into a somnolence
where m/y memory fails. *I* do not know your shoulders
your white neck your shadowed eyes, *I* do not know your

138

palms your exact cheeks, *I* do not know your belly, *I* do not know your breasts your light brown nipples, *I* do not know your back your wide shoulderblades your well-developed buttocks, *I* do not know your brown armpits your pubis your quadrangular fleece, *I* do not know your vulva, *I* do not know your square teeth, *I* do not know your wrists, *I* do not know your sharp voice, *I* do not know your straight nose, *I* do not know your lips, *I* do not know your ears, *I* do not know your hair, *I* am destroyed for you, *I* sleep, *I* dream or else *I* am awoken, *I* breathe, *I* produce cyprine, *I* do not desire you, *I* am forgetful in everything and of everything that concerns you, *I* am not distressed, *I* am calm peaceful flaccid quiet incurious neutral full of composure. *I* am an integral body blocked off from itself, *I* do not hear m/y blood circulate m/y heart beat, *I* do not experience the writhing of m/y viscera, *I* have not the smallest shiver in m/y hair in m/y nape in m/y back or in m/y loins, no throbbing grips m/e in m/y clitoris, *I* am perfectly at ease, *I* am unchoked, *I* am untouched at any point of m/y body and at this point in m/y discourse *I* laugh with fierce insane silent laughter m/y most unknown one, *I* do not bare m/y teeth.

Your mud-fashioned arms rise and fall, *I* see sticking out of their clay the heads and tails of violets, the sky is visible through the holes which indicate the position of the eyes in your face. The smells of wet grass of sprouting tubers of roots of rotting bark of leaf-humus excite m/y sense of smell. Long shudders move and crawl from the roots of m/y hair to the soles of m/y feet. M/y lips slide over your clayey cheeks. Your teeth each with the round-ness and polish of pebbles in a stream fall one by one into m/y mouth. You move gliding on your haunches the iliac bones visible made of hard wood of box or iron-wood. You exhale an acrid sulphur-tasting smoke in which move ochre gleams. Grains of sand issue in thou-sands from your open belly. Your hand covers m/y hand with glistening trails silvered with a kind of drool. *I* adore you like a goddess monstrous with rottenness, you torment m/e with a slow love, desire for you grips m/e with each of your writhings, *I* recall your pale cheeks your sombre gaze your white belly. Then *I* tear the flowers of the daisies in handfuls from the field where they have sprung up high, running *I* come to you, *I* anoint them with saliva, *I* bury them in your breast of soft earth, *I* spit on your thighs, *I* make them shine by rubbing, *I* water your brown back your loins your but-tocks with urine, m/y palms smooth you from above down, *I* venerate you, *I* entreat you, *I* fixedly regard your jaws opening and closing in regular noiseless motion without any sound reaching m/y ears. The over-dry fingers begin to drop from the ends of your arms. A pain grips m/y breast, *I* can no longer bear your gaze m/y

THE GAIT THE WRITHING THE
RUNNING THE LEAPS THE BOUNDS
THE RETREATS THE GESTICULA-
TION THE TREMORS THE CON-
VULSIONS THE THROWING THE
BRAWLING THE TUSSLE THE GRIP-
PING THE HAMMERINGS THE
BLOWS THE EMBRACES THE MOVE-
MENTS THE SWIMMING THE
SHOULDERS THE NECK THE
CHEEKS THE ARMPITS THE BEND
OF THE ELBOWS THE ARMS THE
WRISTS THE HANDS THE FISTS THE
KNUCKLES THE ANKLES THE
KNEES THE CLAVICLES THE EYES

most perfect one, *I* make holes in you with m/y fists, *I* pierce you through and through, *I* curse you in the excess of m/y adoration, *I* dismantle you, *I* tear from your shoulders the great tree-branches all covered with wet leaves, *I* cast you in pieces to the ground, *I* crush your neck your face, *I* make you re-enter the ground whence you spring so as never to return, pouncing on you stiffened dry-eyed fallen from the top of the grave, thus *I* kill you m/y most handsome monster and *I* feel the long worms attacking m/y belly sucking at m/y viscera in succession.

A small rain falls on you multiple dispersed, reaches you cell by cell, the water falls gently, your skin struck multiply tautens, you contract, your loins stir, long movements traverse the length of your back to the throat the plexus the belly, *I* grow, *I* fall on you with redoubled blows, storm lightnings traverse m/e, your skin crackles, your whole body turns to water, *I* spread out over you from top to bottom, *I* spill like a fountain, *I* am poured over you with a great noise, the entire cumulo-nimbus bursts, the mist of water spreads, the shower grows, the water flows in long jets in drops so close as to be indivisible, eddies form at numerous places in your body, your skin becomes hollowed, its elasticity allows craters to develop, at last *I* roll in great globules on your body, *I* hurl m/yself slapping at your shoulders, *I* glide around your iliac bones, *I* make hollows above your breasts, *I* stir around in your belly where the new-formed pools trickle and overflow on to your flanks while eyes closed muscles tense you resist with all your might, *I* begin a brief cry, *I* emit a sudden cry, *I* make a modulation, *I* ululate, suddenly *I* am become a storm, *I* menace you. Then you spring up, you halt, you move, you endeavour to escape, you are still again, you struggle, but already the lightning falls on us in dazzling flashes, flash flash blinding your blood m/y blood, it spills from its conduits, it spreads over our eyes, our hearts begin to throb together in our clitorises.

The women can all see you standing before m/e, looking at m/e, your nostrils inhaling m/y perfume spreading wide whenever you do so and your head is thrown back, the blue sunlight falls on m/y pale blue flowers, the sound of the insects buzzing is suddenly muffled, you approach your hand to touch the petals nearest you but you immediately withdraw it, the silk of m/y flowers tautens spreads on every aspect, m/y calyces closed like a beak like the lips of the vulva are surrounded by a flat blue completely diaphanous aureole. Your fingers splay out, thus they alight on a heap of m/y flowers a cluster, you utter a cry, you lack the impulse to withdraw your hand, your fingertips the skin of your palm are touched by the skin of m/y sleek flowers, then your entire hand plunges into them up to the wrist then the other, now you progress with both hands among the clusters, when finally your whole body advances both arms plunged up to the shoulders in the thick of m/y flowers, *I* take you utterly by surprise, your breasts are touched your throat is touched, your belly is touched, your loins are touched, your buttocks are touched, suddenly the nape of your neck is very heavily burdened with an armful of m/e a massive branch, as you advance the cascade of m/y flowers closes over you, your head too becomes submerged, *I* am terribly tall big strong, you do not complain while *I* trickle over you all flowers all colours all odours. You m/y so desired one legs pliant you submit, knees bent you say O wistaria while *I* surfeit you *ad vitam aeternam*, amen.

I am she who bellows with her three horns, *I* am the triple one, *I* am the formidable benevolent infernal one, *I* am the black the red the white, *I* am the very great tall powerful one she whose noxious breath has poisoned thousands of generations so be it, *I* am seated in the highest of the heavens in the starry circle where dwells Sappho of the violet cheeks, as with her the stars' dazzle pales m/y cheeks, *I* am the sovereign one, *I* thunder with m/y three voices the clamorous the serene the strident, but *I* immediately relinquish m/y indubitably hierarchical position at your arrival, *I* raise you from your kneeling posture, *I* tear your mouth from m/y knees, possessed by a lively fever *I* cast m/yself at your feet from which m/y tongue licks the dust, *I* say blessed art thou among women who art come the first to release m/e from m/y condition glittering maybe but sombre nonetheless because of m/y very great solitude, may you lose the sense of morning and evening of the stupid duality with all that flows therefrom, may you conceive yourself as *I* at last see you over the greatest possible space, may your understanding embrace the complexity of the play of the stars and of the feminine agglomerations, may you yourself in this place strive in a frenzied confrontation whether in the shape of the angel or the shape of the demon, may the music of the spheres envelop your struggle, may you not lose your way in pursuing the stillborn, may the black star crown you finally, giving you to sit at m/y side at the apogee of the figuration of lesbian love m/y most unknown.

Your body is all bristling with its long iron spikes, your every movement makes them clash together, *I* regard you thus, you are immobile bizarre your eyes quite closed, *I* have barely to touch one of the spikes here or there, your skin begins to quiver, rapidly the gooseflesh spreads, it covers your entire body, *I* touch the iron at an increasing number of points, *I* do so as lightly as *I* can, your body comes to life, in short *I* compel you to stir, *I* kiss your eyelids, *I* compel you, *I* order you to look at m/e, when your eyes open opposite m/ine vertigo takes m/e, *I* speed the movement of the wires, *I* press them, *I* push on them, *I* even dig them in places into your muscles, you quiver, you stiffen, you do not cry out, m/y hands do their work all over your body, your mouth uncovers your teeth, your neck tautens, your head falls back, you are seized with a slow soft movement, the

146

bulge of your throat is sucked by m/y mouth, you are agitated by violent tremors, *I* see you all bristling with the metal spikes, you resound, you are seized with frenzied movement, you struggle until *I* fall on you, then we writhe against each other, *I* find m/yself wounded in m/y turn by the wires that pierce you, m/y skin is rapidly avulsed, *I* become red with blood, *I* am flayed from top to bottom of m/y body up to m/y neck, the round muscles the long muscles, all the fibres of m/y muscles laid bare can be enumerated, *I* begin to hiccup, you do not release m/e, you hold m/e against you in such fashion that *I* begin to be transfixed m/y most inexorable one with such insistence that at this point *I* find nothing to say, unless it suffices to state m/y most memorable one that *I* do not seek to escape you.

The kaleidoscope game consists of inserting a handful of yellow blue pink mauve orange green violet flies beneath someone's eyelids, m/ine for instance. They are really

147

tiny flies minute insects, their peculiarity lies in the bizarre intensity of their colours. You place them between m/y eyelid and m/y eyeball despite m/y protestations and laughter. As soon as m/y lids meet hermetically above and below they begin to fidget. The mauve one for instance progresses with extreme slowness, another one yellow let's say begins to describe zigzags, another rotates on the spot, that one's orange, there's one that systematically traverses the interior of the periphery of m/y eye, *I* see the violet one hurl itself incessantly against the skin of m/y eyelid, a pink one gets caught up in a welling tear. The same thing happens in the other eye. When you place your fingertips against m/y closed eyes *I* see them becoming frenzied, they spin round in every direction which makes the colours change rapidly, *I*'ve no time to pay attention to all their formations to all their dispositions. When you press on m/y eyeballs even when you press very lightly a Brownian movement occurs between m/y eyes and m/y lids, but since the flies are protected by the moistness of the ambient medium there is no mishap, at a given moment the tingling of their multiple feet the suction of their thousands of microscopic suckers irritate m/y cornea, it's impossible for m/e to retain them any longer, you collect them m/y beloved on a sheet of glass where m/y tears fall.

I am in the cold stream at high noon. M/y gums are gashed, they are shall we say more or less sawn through by the water, it makes a cut a precise incision right across m/y mouth, m/y teeth are laid bare, *I* draw up *I* suck in the cold, m/y whole face is racked with pain. *I* crawl in the mud and the weed, there *I* reach you m/y serenest one, your whole body is icy quite flat gigantic distorted by the movement of the water. *I* stand before you, m/y two hands grasp you round your waist, thus *I* hold you beneath the surface, *I* see your eyes, *I* see your cheeks, *I* see your mouth, *I* see your shoulders, *I* see your arms your legs. Despite the dazzling sunlight the water solidifies progressively on your body and around m/y legs, *I* agitate them incessantly to prevent excessive hardening. Around us the water is changing state as far as *I* can see. A thick layer of ice now extends above you, beneath only a slight current moves, your horizontally extended arms and legs are stirred from time to time. When the solidification of the water appears to m/e sufficiently advanced for you to be no longer able to break free, *I* exert traction on the middle of your body, *I* thrust you against the bottom of the lake, so doing *I* raise m/yself wrenching m/yself from the ice, at a given moment *I* find m/yself lying face downward just above you engaged in looking at you through the transparency, the water stirred up by m/y movements overflows from below on to the crust of ice where it is broken, here where *I* am engaged in watching you it is thick enough, yet *I* do not stir, *I* note that your movements are more rapid than if they were excited solely by the now undoubtedly nonexistent current at the place you occupy, you become agitated however, you struggle, m/y eyes applied to the surface of the ice see yours open on the other side, you look at m/e, you raise your hands, you push with all your might against the layer above you, *I* hear it crack while *I* let the water round m/e set and freeze, *I* burden you with all m/y weight lying on you, *I* become numbed in m/y entire body but *I* remain here, *I* allow m/yself to become imprisoned so as to look at you to become increasingly immobile, you become rigid, you shine in the sun in the block of ice m/y best beloved, you are borne by no current.

When you force m/e to open m/y mouth you disclose m/y sawlike teeth. You say that you feel unafraid of this unprepossessing aspect of m/y person. You allow m/e to draw you to m/e to slash greedily at your throat the nape of your neck, you allow m/e to lay bare the muscles

of your cheeks, you allow m/e to incise the whole length
of your arms inside and out, you allow m/e to sever your
breasts whose blood spurts parallel to splash into m/y
eyes, you allow m/e to make an opening all round your
belly, you allow m/e to see your viscera all steaming
yellow white green, the duodenum the small intestine the
large intestine, now *I* hear their loud noises undisguised,
you allow m/e to touch your bladder, you allow m/e to
flay both your thighs, your sex is intact, already *I* am
covered in your blood, m/y face m/y hands m/y bust
m/y hair are all sticky. You barely slightly paler magni-
ficent very regal you laugh, you tell m/e that *I* am
impotent to make you suffer.

When after the dawn the sun is blinding you are revealed
to m/e in all your glory skin made of scales in the
dazzling light blood vaginal juice long congealed strands
on your belly dried spittle on your cheeks marbled skin
covered with stains black eyes rimmed with black cheeks
black, desire for you grips m/e incessantly when head
rolling dragging your mass of hair you are caught by

151

the sun, m/y lips shoot, they become an elongated gutter, the upper lip clings to the lower lip, they fuse, the length of m/y single lip is soon such that it coils on itself forming a spiral crozier, it is a sucker a very narrow trunk, *I* apply it lightly to your throat your shoulders your nipples your belly your vulva, you sigh in your sleep, m/y flexible antennae palpate in your hair in your ears on your eyelids, *I* suck up with m/y trunk all the fine particles which have accumulated on your skin, *I* absorb the juices while *I* grasp you between m/y six feet, the first two surround your head, the others immobilize your pelvis against which *I* thrust m/y segmented abdomen, some of your convulsions split m/y chitinous skeleton. Through the facets of m/y eyes *I* have no unitary vision of your body, you are diversified, you are different, *I* suddenly embody signals from your arms fragments of your belly part of a shoulder one of your labia, *I* see you everywhere at once, an intoxication grips m/e, *I* apprehend you in innumerable morsels, *I* lose m/yself in your geography, m/y trunk palpates you searchingly, clinging to you thus by m/y six feet *I* begin m/y delectable one to flap m/y wings against your back, a fine powder of a dazzling blue spreads over your shoulders into your hair, m/y movement gains effect, *I* disengage you from the ground, *I* lift you up, *I* tear you away, *I* carry you off flying sound asleep above the sea.

THE MOUTH THE LIPS THE JAWS
THE EARS THE RIDGES OF THE EYE-
BROWS THE TEMPLES THE NOSE
THE CHEEKS THE CHIN THE FORE-
HEAD THE EYELIDS THE COM-
PLEXION THE ANKLE THE THIGHS
THE HAMS THE CALVES THE HIPS
THE VULVA THE BACK THE CHEST
THE BREASTS THE SHOULDER-
BLADES THE BUTTOCKS THE
ELBOWS THE LEGS THE TOES THE
FEET THE HEELS THE LOINS THE
NAPE THE THROAT THE HEAD THE
INSTEPS THE GROINS THE TONGUE
THE OCCIPUT THE SPINE THE
FLANKS THE NAVEL THE PUBIS
THE LESBIAN BODY.

M/y cells enlarge beneath your fingers m/y most atrocious one. M/y skin is covered with ocelli red light-brown plaques, the globules of the cell-nuclei enlarged thousands of times provoke considerable perturbations, they transgress the nuclear membranes, they roll around in the cytoplasm of their cells, they emerge from it by brute force, *I* see enormous quantities of shining nucleoli leaping all around m/e, some have dragged with them the nuclei in which they were imprisoned, from m/y skin there emerge bodies comparable for the most part to glass marbles others to taws, bubbles form continually at the surface of m/y body touched by your fingers, *I* see them burst silently on m/y arms in long orange green spurts, m/y skin is entirely covered with water, the expelled cytoplasm flows, *I* stream, depressions wells are dug, your fingers plunge therein precipitately abandoning them for others newly-formed, then eddies of air rush in, a slight noise a hissing susurrations become perceptible, as the phenomenon accelerates and continues the sound becomes a series of bellowings of whistlings ceasing abruptly then beginning again, *I* am the site of a great hubbub, thus *I* become increasingly immobile while you m/y so ferocious one m/y frenzied one you have an incomparable speed, you come and go in m/y widened pores in m/y alveoli in m/y cavities in m/y furrows in

m/y trenches in m/y crevices, you mine m/e, m/y
surface caves in, step by step it affects m/y entire body
m/y muscles m/y blood m/y bones m/y vital organs
m/y substances until decomposition is complete. When
you stop m/y darling, you will have spongy matter on
your hands and on your arms viscosities pitch putrescence
blood lymph bile you m/y most intact.

I see the sun shining between your ribs. The sky of an
intense blue is also visible in certain intervals of their
arrangement. M/y head is placed on the ground against
you resting at the level of your seventh right rib. At this
point the bulge of your thorax is already beginning to
diminish following the descending scale of your ribs.
Had *I* to come here thousands of times *I* should still run
to the bend in the path from which *I* can see your
skeleton all white lying on the hilltop. *I* can make out

the parallel disposition of your ribs from afar. As *I* approach *I* can distinguish your skull your pelvis your humeri your ulnae your radii your femora your tibiae. You are lying on your shoulderblades and on your vertebrae, your iliac bones are prominent. *I* fling m/yself down beside you m/y best-beloved, *I* kiss the phalanges of your hands, *I* look sideways at you just as when we used to run a long while on the moors of the island and fling ourselves down all heated breathless you perfectly still watching the sky, now your orbits are exposed nose indented, your small square teeth prolonged by their bosses over your jawbones. The pink flowers of the heather are visible in the spaces between your bones and all around you. Once again *I* am seized with the desire to take you in m/y arms to kiss your eyes your mouth your clavicles your sternum. Or else *I* hold you very close m/y legs against your legs your arms around m/y neck, *I* stay still even when night is come when the chill and the dew make m/e shiver when no warmth from you reaches m/e while *I* am in life while *I* wait for the cold to overcome m/e so as to remain here with you m/y so adorable one in this cemetery in the open air m/y bones mingled with yours.

A solitary moon is shining while *I* await you beneath the tall sorb-apple tree. The white flowers of the tree are brightly illuminated by its violet light. *I* have hidden m/yself to watch you arrive. The sea is rough, it is visible in the less dark places under the light of the moon there where violet pools incessantly form and change. *I* cannot make out the innumerable lights of the fisherwomen's boats. Yet they must have left port as the colour of the beacons indicates. You do not come. Some of the women pass close to m/e without seeing m/e, they sing, they dance as they go, their voices rise and break off abruptly, one of them plays a musical instrument, a flute held cross-wise *I* believe. They halt under the sorb-apple and kiss each other on the mouth one after the other, then all together forming a single mouth wish each other a happy night. A gust of wind causes numerous white mauve petals to fall on their hair and shoulders. They repeat a phrase stressing the sound s, *I* vow by the tall sorb-apple or something like that. The second moon becomes visible in its turn. Its colour is orange. Very rapidly it covers two-thirds of the path of the violet moon. Their two spheres are identical in size. But one moves more rapidly than the other. The colours they emit do not blend. When they are next to one another they are prolonged by two luminous cones one violet the other orange, they are superimposed at the brief moment when they intersect. You do not come. Unless you are actually among them here engaged in singing and dancing. *I* fling out both m/y arms as quickly as *I* can, *I* grab someone whom *I* drag across the gleaming masses of the rhododendrons towards m/e, *I* look at her, *I* touch her bare skin, she looks at m/e laughing, it is not you m/y best-beloved her hair is another colour red or perhaps orange in the moonlight, her eyes are a stranger's, she takes m/e by the neck and kisses m/e, *I* do not restrain her departure. *I* catch five of them in this way, one is fair her skin is white, the other three are dark their skin is black, one alone has the property of retaining the gleams of both moons. All the women make mocking gestures at m/e, one bites m/y neck, another drools her saliva into one of m/y ears, another feigning to depart leaps on m/y back, her feet digging into m/y loins she makes of m/e a giraffe to carry her, now *I* hear them singing about someone who confuses essence and appearance. *I* spit on the ground, *I* fling out m/y arms for the last time, it is you you cheat whom *I* haul in at last silent cold addressing m/e saying that *I* have been kissed enough for the night, *I* swear by the tall sorb-apple that *I* shan't be caught again.

Is there no Archimedea to be encountered anywhere that
the baths are so perfumed with *eau de Chypre*? *I* never
see you in the cool dark-blue pine-groves which flank
the island shore, but there in the gloom m/y eyes relax
from the daylight's dazzle the weight of m/y arms m/y
legs burdens m/e no longer when *I* rest them on the
pine needles, the mingled odours of the warm resin and
the sea lead m/e to seek you lying beside m/e. But in
fact you are at the baths, it's there *I* rejoin you, you are
engaged in floating flat on the warm water, *I* look at
you, your body stands out against the orange and violet
mosaics, *I* anoint m/yself with oils and essences, *I* swim,
I press m/y belly against your back, *I* sing, *I* float the
now empty perfume vases, I fill them with handfuls of
water, they remain at the surface though half-full, then
I add the water in smaller and smaller amounts, slowly
they submerge all round you, they are full to the brim,
they sink and yet they remain at the surface, a single
drop would make them founder. *I* begin the game all
over again several times. Suddenly emerging from your
torpor you empty them as fast as possible, you place
them on the surface of the water, you cause m/e to
observe that a body immersed in a liquid sustains a
vertical thrust directed from below upwards, that m/y
dearest is manifest to anyone who spends three-quarters

of the day plunged in the water, but you insist, you say that the thrust may be measured in terms of the weight of water displaced, you say that you have discovered therein a fundamental law of our physical universe, at these words *I* can no longer contain m/y laughter, *I* sink therefore, *I* emerge to thank the Blessed One the thrice august since you woman of little faith do not think of so doing.

She has let herself be caught in the race tackled by you losing. Now she stands between you and m/e eyes bandaged she is laughing. *I* touch her shoulders her breasts her neck her hair. You hold her with her back against you. At a given moment you lift her under the armpits while *I* grasp her legs. She is borne thus towards the square where the gallery of your dwelling opens. In the gallery there are similar groups with bearers and borne. From time to time a single bearer carries someone stretched out between her arms. It is the day of the pursuit. It is carried out by drawing lots. The eyes of those who run are bandaged. They depart at the trumpet's signal straight before them in the most open space of the island. They can run at full speed without risk.

But those who escape their pursuers are rare. Stones roots make them stumble and slow them down. Or else the unaccustomedness of moving so rapidly without looking. The place where you live is a sort of enlargement of the gallery, semicircular, opening on the sea completely open with a great circulation of wind of air of sound. It is there that the pursued has cast herself down. She attempts to rise then to flee. You hold her against the paved floor. *I* remain lying down. The sweat streams on m/y cheeks on m/y back. The sea-breeze cools m/e. *I* ask her name, but enraged at having lost the race she refuses to answer. *I* watch her struggling in your arms, *I* hear her calling for m/y help, *I* roll against her to try to grasp her arms her shoulders or her legs. Finally she bursts out laughing, her muscles relax, she asks for her bandage to be removed so she may see where she is. You m/y incomparable one you kiss her cheeks and mouth. Night falls. One can hear the sea.

Your arms of white-hot steel burn m/y arm, m/y most fiery one, the fingers of your hand make the flesh of m/y fingers splutter, m/y nails shrivel, m/y skin flakes, falls in grey ash. Yet your contacts with m/y body multiply, you regard m/e your jet teeth clenched, your burning breath reaches m/y lips m/y tongue m/y palate, soon *I* am gripped by thirst. Under your mouth m/y ears shrivel, m/y breasts m/y thighs m/y buttocks m/y back m/y vulva char. A thick malodorous smoke surrounds m/e. The more *I* shrivel the more *I* shrink, the more you grow and develop, your shoulders are immense, your hair of tin floats outspread, your arms and hands grow longer, your head swells, you dominate m/e by your sheer size. M/y muscles begin to roast, the fire smoulders in places, ravages in others, it is fanned by your feverish movements, it attacks m/y flesh everywhere, m/y blood issuing all solidified at various breaches falls to the ground as clots of black red phosphorescent stone. You chew m/e up, your lips of radiant tungsten perforate m/e, the long muscles of m/y forearms of m/y thighs appear through the burst skin. Under the influence of the intense combustion certain vital organs m/y liver lungs heart abruptly petrify and begin to fall. M/y hair coils in long streamers on your thighs, your hands are filled with it, they set it ablaze and char it. M/y bones laid bare become incandescent then fall in powder. M/y clitoris detached from its burning hood rolls glinting at your feet ready to adorn one of your fingers in the setting of a ring. M/y eyes offered to you on a plate are, you say, delicious. M/y hair fallen in tufts sticks in your throat choking you, *I* melt *I* disintegrate *I* am burnt up m/y wretched mistress you devour m/e too precipitately.

There where the sun can melt the wings of wax you bear
m/e O radiant Félise in the wavering journey you under-
take with some temerity. It did not suffice for you to
transform m/e into a flying-machine two pairs of wings
attached to m/y shoulders, and in fact *I* do fly, you have
taken great pains to find the right viaticum to give m/e
strength. That is why you have chosen to be on the
journey holding m/e by the neck borne on m/y arms.
Thus you encourage m/e with your words your kisses
your honeyed saliva in m/y mouth to redouble m/y
efforts at intervals to distance m/yself from the island.
Despite everything *I* weaken, *I* do not know when this
will prove fatal. At noon maybe when m/y breast exposed m/y skin burnt by the sun *I* am at the end of m/y
ability m/y so black one to carry you in m/y arms. Or
else at the hour of the siesta when all the women are to
be seen recumbent in the shade-filled pine-groves while
I struggle with you against the laws of gravity. *I* have
begun to melt. You lick m/e all over, all m/y hairs stuck
to your teeth, you suck up m/y boiling eyes, you squeeze
m/y breast with one powerful arm while with the
other you hold m/e against you in m/y now slackening
flight. But you cannot sustain m/e. Now instead of rising
I fall legs together. M/y arms release you. Not one of
those eagles with the menacing eyes comes to support

163

you. *I* am the first to succumb, *I* fall backwards m/y wings broken you following m/e closely headfirst the women all very far-off down below standing watching the most irremediable fall of all, may the goddesses ensure that *I* that you will be able to hear their cries on reaching the sea.

It is the women of group number seven who are the mountebanks. Their capers their gesticulations their juggling their exclamations their songs their garments made of a patchwork of bright colours produce an eddy in the midst of the assembly. An increasingly large circle forms around them. Each bears the number seven marked on the front of her shoulders. You are one of them. Among the spectators *I* can like everyone else contemplate your neck your slender nape the effect produced by the violet inscription of the number seven on your translucent skin.

You hold a musical instrument in your hand, a guitar it seems to m/e. Your mouth utters modulations and stridencies. One of the women marks the rapid rhythm of the music by beating the skins of a tom-tom. You do not look at m/e. Your eyes are turned in the direction of the sea which prolongs the principal square of the island, it is visible as a pastel blue between the snowy-flowering cherry-trees specified in the architecture of their branches and their inflorescences. A sudden gust of wind shakes them causing them to shed a great quantity of petals, their slow fall continues between the now stationary trees. At a given moment the song of the group number seven rises loud, so well known to all the women that it is taken up in unison over and over again. The circle yields, the troupers of group number seven lend their balls to those who wish to juggle. Capers are cut by the majority of the assembly. All are to be seen head-over-heels between the stalls the flowerbeds the fountains. Laughs shouts collisions are heard. Someone begins a standing double somersault. The smell of pralines mingled with that of flowers perceptible through the changes of the wind is very strong. *I* seek you m/y radiant one across the throng.